The Best of the World's Classics

VOL. VI

GREAT BRITAIN AND IRELAND—IV

1801—1909

RUSKIN

DICKENS

THACKERAY

DARWIN

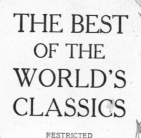

THE BEST
OF THE
WORLD'S
CLASSICS

RESTRICTED
TO PROSE

HENRY CABOT LODGE
EDITOR-IN-CHIEF

FRANCIS W. HALSEY
ASSOCIATE EDITOR

With an Introduction, Biographical and Explanatory
Notes, etc.

IN TEN VOLUMES

Vol. VI
GREAT BRITAIN AND IRELAND—IV

FUNK & WAGNALLS COMPANY
NEW YORK AND LONDON

CONTENTS

CONTENTS

CONTENTS

CONTENTS

CONTENTS

GREAT BRITAIN AND IRELAND—IV

1801—1909

JOHN HENRY NEWMAN

Born in 1801, died in 1890; son of a banker; educated at Oxford; a Fellow of Oriel in 1822, where he was associated with Dr. Pusey; made a voyage to the Mediterranean in 1832-33, returning from which he wrote "Lead, Kindly Light"; joined the Oxford movement in 1833, writing many of the "tracts for the times"; formally joined the Catholic Church in 1845; established an Oratory in 1849; published "Lectures" in 1850, the "Apologia" in 1864, "Grammar of Ascent" in 1870; made a cardinal in 1879.

I

THE BEGINNINGS OF TRACTARIANISM[1]

DURING the first years of my residence at Oriel, tho proud of my college, I was not quite at home there. I was very much alone, and I used often to take my daily walk by myself. I recollect once meeting Dr. Copleston, then Provost, with one of the Fellows. He turned round, and with the kind courteousness which sat so well on him, made me a bow and said, *Nunquam minus solus, quam cum solus*. At that time, indeed (from 1823), I had the intimacy of my dear and true friend Dr. Pusey, and could not fail to admire and revere a soul so devoted to the cause of religion, so full of good works, so faithful in his affections; but he left residence when I was

[1] From the "Apologia pro Vita Sua."

3

getting to know him well. As to Dr. Whately [2] himself, he was too much my superior to allow of my being at my ease with him; and to no one in Oxford at this time did I open my heart fully and familiarly. But things changed in 1826. At that time I became one of the tutors of my college, and this gave me position; besides, I had written one or two essays which had been well received. I began to be known. I preached my first University sermon. Next year I was one of the public examiners for the B. A. degree. In 1828 I became vicar of St. Mary's. It was to me like the feeling of spring weather after winter; and, if I may so speak, I came out of my shell. I remained out of it until 1841.

The two persons who knew me best at that time are still alive, beneficed clergymen, no longer my friends. They could tell better than any one else what I was in those days. From this time my tongue was, as it were, loosened, and I spoke spontaneously and without effort. One of the two, a shrewd man, said of me, I have been told, "Here is a Fellow who, when he is silent, will never begin to speak, and when he once begins to speak will never stop." It was at this time that I began to have influence, which steadily increased for a course of years. I gained upon my pupils, and was in particular intimate and affectionate with two of our Probationer Fellows, Robert Isaac Wilberforce

[2] Richard Whately, Bampton lecturer at Oxford in 1822; principal of St. Albans Hall in 1825; afterward Archbishop of Dublin; best known for his "Logic" and "Christian Evidences." When Newman met him, he was already famous for his "Historical Doubts Relative to Napoleon Bonaparte," which had been published in 1814.

4

(afterward Archdeacon), and Richard Hurrell Froude.[3] Whately then, an acute man, perhaps saw around me the signs of an incipient party of which I was not conscious myself. And thus we discern the first elements of that movement afterward called Tractarian. The true and primary author of it, however, as is usual with great motive powers, was out of sight. Having carried off, as a mere boy, the highest honors of the University, he had turned from the admiration which haunted his steps, and sought for a better and holier satisfaction in pastoral work in the country.

Need I say that I am speaking of John Keble?[4] The first time that I was in a room with him was on the occasion of my election to a Fellowship at Oriel, when I was sent for into the Tower, to shake hands with the Provost and Fellows. How is that hour fixt in my memory after the changes of forty-two years; forty-two this very day on which I write! I have lately had a letter in my hands which I sent at the time to my great friend, John William Bowden, with whom I passed almost exclusively my undergraduate years. "I had to hasten to the Tower,"

[3] A brother of James Anthony Froude. Richard Hurrell Froude's influence on the founding of the Tractarian movement was strong. He cooperated with Newman in writing the "Lyra Apostolica." His health had long been delicate, when in 1836 he died. His "Remains" were published in the following year, with a preface by Newman. Three of the "Tracts for the Times" were by Froude.

[4] Keble, one of the chief promoters of the Oxford movement, will long be remembered as author of "The Christian Year," published in 1827. For ten years he was Professor of Poetry at Oxford. Three of the "Tracts for the Times" were by him. He was Newman's senior by eight years.

I say to him, "to receive the congratulations of all the Fellows. I bore it till Keble took my hand, and then felt so abashed and unworthy of the honor done to me, that I seemed desirous of quite sinking into the ground." His had been the first name which I had heard spoken of, with reverence rather than admiration, when I came up to Oxford. When one day I was walking in High Street with my dear earliest friend just mentioned, with what eagerness did he cry out, "There's Keble!" and with what awe did I look at him! Then at another time I heard a Master of Arts of my college give an account how he had just then had occasion to introduce himself on some business to Keble, and how gentle, courteous, and unaffected Keble had been, so as almost to put him out of countenance. Then, too, it was reported, truly or falsely, how a rising man of brilliant reputation, the present Dean of St. Paul's, Dr. Milman, admired and loved him, adding, that somehow he was strangely unlike any one else. However, at the time when I was elected Fellow of Oriel, he was not in residence, and he was shy of me for years, in consequence of the marks which I bore upon me of the Evangelical and Liberal schools, at least so I have ever thought. Hurrell Froude brought us together about 1828; it is one of the sayings preserved in his "Remains"—"Do you know the story of the murderer who had done one good thing in his life? Well, if I was ever asked what good thing I had ever done, I should say I had brought Keble and Newman to understand each other."

II

ON HIS SUBMISSION TO THE CATHOLIC CHURCH [5]

I HAD one final advance of mind to accomplish, and one final step to take. That further advance of mind was to be able honestly to say that I was certain of the conclusions at which I had already arrived. That further step, imperative when such certitude was attained, was my submission to the Catholic Church.

This submission did not take place till two full years after the resignation of my living in September 1843; nor could I have made it at an earlier date, without doubt and apprehension; that is, with any true conviction of mind or certitude.

In the interval, of which it remains to speak— viz., between the autumns of 1843 and 1845—I was in lay communion with the Church of England: attending its services as usual, and abstaining altogether from intercourse with Catholics, from their places of worship, and from those religious rites and usages, such as the

[5] From the "Apologia." Newman, for many years, had held to the possibility of English churchmen maintaining a middle ground between the Catholic Church and Protestantism, but in 1843 he abandoned this hope, resigning his living, and in 1845 formally entered the Catholic Church. He says in the "Apologia" that "from the end of 1841, I was on my death-bed as regards my membership with the Anglican church, tho at the time I became aware of it only by degrees."

Invocation of Saints, which are characteristics of their creed. I did all this on principle; for I never could understand how a man could be of two religions at once.

What I have to say about myself between these two autumns I shall almost confine to this one point—the difficulty I was in as to the best mode of revealing the state of my mind to my friends and others, and how I managed to reveal it.

Up to January, 1842, I had not disclosed my state of unsettlement to more than three persons. . . . To two of them, intimate and familiar companions, in the autumn of 1839; to the third—an old friend too, whom I have also named above—I suppose when I was in great distress of mind upon the affair of the Jerusalem Bishopric. In May, 1843, I made it known, as has been seen, to the friend by whose advice I wished, as far as possible, to be guided. To mention it on set purpose to any one, unless indeed I was asking advice, I should have felt to be a crime. If there is anything that was abhorrent to me, it was the scattering doubts, and unsettling consciences without necessity. A strong presentiment that my existing opinions would ultimately give way, and that the grounds of them were unsound, was not a sufficient warrant for disclosing the state of my mind. I had no guarantee yet, that that presentiment would be realized. Supposing I were crossing ice, which came right in my way, which I had good reasons for considering sound, and which I saw numbers before me crossing in safety, and supposing a stranger from the bank, in a voice of authority and in an earnest tone, warned me that it was dangerous, and then was silent—I think I should be startled, and should look about me anxiously, but I think too that I should go on, till I had better grounds for doubt; and such was my state, I believe, till the end of 1842. Then again, when my dissatisfaction became greater, it was hard at first to determine the point of time when it was too strong to suppress with propriety. Certitude of course is a point, but doubt is a progress: I was not near certitude yet. Certitude is a reflex action; it is to know that one knows. Of that I believe I was not possest, till close upon my reception into the Catholic Church. Again, a practical, effective doubt is a point too; but who can easily ascertain it for himself? Who can determine when it is that the scales in the balance of opinion begin to turn, and what was a greater probability in behalf of a belief becomes a positive doubt against it?

In considering this question in its bearing upon my conduct in 1843, my own simple answer to my great difficulty had been, Do what your present state of opinion requires in the light of duty, and let that doing tell; speak by acts. This I had done; my first act of the year had been in February. After three months' deliberation I had published my retractation of the violent charges which I had made against Rome: I could not be wrong in doing so much as this; but I did no more at the time: I did not retract my Anglican teaching. My second act had been in September in the same year: after much sorrowful lingering and hesitation, I had resigned my Living. I tried indeed, before I did so, to keep Littlemore for myself, even tho it was still to

remain an integral part of St. Mary's.[6] I had
given to it a church and a sort of parsonage;
I had made it a parish, and I loved it: I thought
in 1843 that perhaps I need not forfeit my existing relations toward it. I could indeed submit to become a curate at will of another; but I
hoped an arrangement was possible by which,
while I had the curacy, I might have been my
own master in serving it. I had hoped an exception might have been made in my favor, under
the circumstances; but I did not gain my request.
Perhaps I was asking what was impracticable,
and it is well for me that it was so.

These had been my two acts of the year, and
I said, "I can not be wrong in making them;
let that follow which must follow in the thoughts
of the world about me, when they see what I
do." And as time went on, they fully answered
my purpose. What I felt it a simple duty to do,
did create a general suspicion about me, without
such responsibility as would be involved in my
initiating any direct act for the sake of creating
it. Then, when friends wrote me on the subject,
I either did not deny or I confest my state of
mind, according to the character and need of
their letters. Sometimes in the case of intimate
friends, whom I should otherwise have been

[6] St. Mary's was the church of the University of Oxford,
Newman being its vicar. Littlemore was an outlying place
attached to St. Mary's and to which Newman withdrew
on leaving Oxford in 1842. Here, with several young men
who had attached themselves to his fortunes, he established himself in a building which came to be known as
"the Littlemore Monastery." It was here that Newman
passed the three years of meditation and anxiety which
preceded his final decision to join the Roman Church.

leaving in ignorance of what others knew on every side of them, I invited the question.

And here comes in another point for explanation. While I was fighting in Oxford for the Anglican Church, then indeed I was very glad to make converts; and tho I never broke away from that rule of my mind (as I may call it) of which I have already spoken, of finding disciples rather than seeking them, yet that I made advances to others in a special way, I have no doubt; this came to an end, however, as soon as I fell into misgivings as to the true ground to be taken in the controversy. For then, when I gave up my place in the movement, I ceased from any such proceedings; and my utmost endeavor was to tranquillize such persons, especially those who belonged to the new school, as were unsettled in their religious views, and as I judged, hasty in their conclusions. This went on till 1843; but at that date, as soon as I turned my face Romeward, I gave up, as far as ever was possible, the thought of, in any respect and in any shape, acting upon others. Then I myself was simply my own concern. How could I in any sense direct others, who had to be guided in so momentous a matter myself? How could I be considered in a position, even to say a word to them, one way or the other? How could I presume to unsettle them as I was unsettled, when I had no means of bringing them out of such unsettlement? And if they were unsettled already, how could I point to them a place of refuge, when I was not sure that I should choose it for myself? My only line, my only duty, was to keep simply to my own case. I recollected

Pascal's words, "Je mourrai seul" [I will die alone]. I deliberately put out of my thoughts all other works and claims, and said nothing to any one, unless I was obliged.

But this brought upon me a great trouble. In the newspapers there were continual reports about my intentions; I did not answer them: presently strangers or friends wrote, begging to be allowed to answer them; and if I still kept to my resolution and said nothing, then I was thought to be mysterious, and a prejudice was excited against me. But what was far worse, there were a number of tender, eager hearts, of whom I knew nothing at all, who were watching me, wishing to think as I thought, and to do as I did, if they could but find it out; who in consequence were distrest that in so solemn a matter they could not see what was coming, and who heard reports about me this way or that, on a first day and on a second; and felt the weariness of waiting, and the sickness of delayed hope, and did not understand that I was as perplexed as they were, and being of more sensitive complexion of mind than myself, they were made ill by the suspense. And they too, of course, for the time thought me mysterious and inexplicable. I ask their pardon as far as I was really unkind to them. . . .

I left Oxford for good on Monday, February 23d, 1846. On the Saturday and Sunday before, I was in my house at Littlemore simply by myself, as I had been for the first day or two when I had originally taken possession of it. I slept on Sunday night at my dear friend's, Mr. Johnson's, at the Observatory. Various friends came to see the last of me: Mr. Copeland, Mr. Church, Mr. Buckle, Mr. Pattison, and Mr. Lewis. Dr. Pusey too came up to take leave of me; and I called on Dr. Ogle, one of my very oldest friends, for he was my private tutor when I was an undergraduate. In him I took leave of my first college, Trinity, which was so dear to me, and which held on its foundation so many who had been kind to me both when I was a boy, and all through my Oxford life. Trinity had never been unkind to me. There used to be much snapdragon growing on the walls opposite my freshman's rooms there; and I had for years taken it as the emblem of my own perpetual residence, even unto death, in my University.

On the morning of the 23d I left the Observatory. I have never seen Oxford since, excepting its spires as they are seen from the railway.

III

OF ATHENS AS A TRUE UNIVERSITY [7]

IF we would know what a university is, considered in its most elementary idea, we must betake ourselves to the first and most beautiful home of European civilization, to the bright and beautiful Athens,—Athens, whose schools drew to her bosom, and then sent back to the business of life, the youth of the Western world for a long thousand years. Seated on the verge of

[7] From Volume III of the "Historical Sketches."

the continent, the city seemed hardly suited for
the duties of a central metropolis of knowledge;
yet what it lost in convenience of approach, it
gained in its neighborhood to the traditions of
the mysterious East, and in the loveliness of the
region in which it lay. Hither, then, as to a
sort of ideal land, where all the archetypes of
the great and the fair were found in substantial
being, and all departments of truth explored, and
all diversities of intellectual power exhibited;
where taste and philosophy were majestically
enthroned as in a royal court; where there was
no sovereignty but that of mind, and no nobility but that of genius; where professors were
rulers and princes did homage,—hither flocked
continually from the very corners of the *orbis
terrarum*, the many-tongued generation, just rising or just risen into manhood, in order to gain
wisdom.

Pisistratus [8] had at an early age discovered and
nursed the infant genius of his people, and
Cimon,[9] after the Persian war, had given it a
home; that war had established the naval
supremacy of Athens; she had become an imperial state; and the Ionians, bound to her by
the double chain of kindred and of subjection,
were importing into her both their merchandise
and their civilization. The arts and philosophy
of the Asiatic Court were easily carried across

[8] Pisistratus flourished from 605 B.C. until 527. He was
a friend of Solon, but usurped supreme power in 560; was
twice expelled and then restored to power. He is usually
credited with a notable systematic attempt to preserve the
works of Homer.

[9] Cimon died in 449 B.C. He was a son of Miltiades
and defeated the Persians on both sea and land in 466.

the sea, and there was Cimon, as I have said, with his ample fortune, ready to receive them with due honor. Not content with patronizing their profession, he built the first of those noble porticoes, of which we hear so much in Athens, and he formed the groves, which in process of time formed the celebrated academy. Planting is one of the most graceful, as in Athens it was one of the most beneficent, of employments. Cimon took in hand the wild wood, pruned and drest it, and laid it out with handsome walks and welcome fountains. Nor, while hospitable to the authors of the city's civilization, was he ungrateful to the instruments of her prosperity. His trees extended their cool, umbrageous branches over the merchants who assembled in the Agora, for many generations.

Those merchants certainly had deserved that act of bounty; for all the while their ships had been carrying forth the intellectual fame of Athens to the Western world. Then commenced what may be called her university existence. Pericles, who succeeded Cimon, both in the government and in the patronage of art, is said by Plutarch to have entertained the idea of making Athens the capital of federated Greece; in this he failed; but his encouragement of such men as Phidias and Anaxagoras led the way to her acquiring a far more lasting sovereignty over a far wider empire. Little understanding the sources of her own greatness, Athens would go to war; peace is the interest of a seat of commerce and the arts; but to war she went: yet to her whether peace or war mattered not. The political power of Athens waned and disappeared; kingdoms rose and fell, centuries rolled away;—they did but bring fresh triumphs to the city of the poet and the sage. There at length the swarthy Moor and Spaniard were seen to meet the blue-eyed Gaul; and the Cappadocian, late subject to Mithridates, gazed without alarm at the haughty conquering Roman. Revolution after revolution passed over the face of Europe, as well as of Greece, but still she was there,—Athens, the city of the mind, as radiant, as splendid, as delicate, as young, as ever she had been.

Many a more fruitful coast or isle is washed by the blue Ægean, many a spot is there more beautiful or sublime to see, many a territory more ample; but there was one charm in Attica, which in the same perfection was nowhere else. The deep pastures of Arcadia, the plain of Argos, the Thessalian Vale, these had not the gift; Bœotia, which lay to its immediate north, was notorious for the very want of it. The heavy atmosphere of that Bœotia might be good for vegetation, but it was associated in popular belief with the dulness of the Bœotian intellect; on the contrary, the special purity, elasticity, clearness, and salubrity of the air of Attica, fit concomitant and emblem of its genius, did that for it which earth did not;—it brought out every bright line and tender shade of the landscape over which it was spread, and would have illuminated the face even of a more barren and rugged country.

A confined triangle, perhaps fifty miles its greatest length, and thirty its greatest breadth; two elevated rocky barriers meeting at an angle;

three prominent mountains commanding the plain,—Parnes, Pentelicus, and Hymettus; an unsatisfactory soil; some streams, not always full;—such is about the report which the agent of a London company would have made of Attica. He would report that the climate was mild, the hills were limestone; there was plenty of good marble; more pasture than at first survey might have been expected, sufficient certainly for sheep and goats; fisheries productive; silver mines once, but long since worked out; figs, fair; oil, first-rate; olives in profusion. But what he would not think of noting down was, that that olive-tree was so choice in nature and so noble in shape, that it excited a religious veneration, and that it took so kindly to the light soil as to expand into woods upon the open plain, and to climb up and fringe the hills. He would not think of writing word to his employer, how that clear air, of which I have spoken, brought out, yet blended and subdued, the colors on the marble, till they had a softness and harmony, for all their richness, which in a picture looks exaggerated, yet is after all within the truth. He would not tell how that same delicate and brilliant atmosphere freshened up the pale olive, until the olive forgot its monotony, and its cheek glowed like the arbutus or beech of the Umbrian Hills. He would say nothing of the thyme and thousand fragrant herbs which carpeted Hymettus; he would hear nothing of the hum of its bees, nor take much account of the rare flavor of its honey, since Sozo and Minorca were sufficient for the English demand.

He would look over the Ægean from the
height he had ascended; he would follow with
his eye the chain of islands, which, starting
from the Sunian headland, seemed to offer the
fabled divinities of Attica, when they would
visit their Ionian cousins, a sort of viaduct
thereto across the sea; but that fancy would not
occur to him, nor any admiration of the dark
violet billows with their white edges down below; nor of those graceful, fanlike jets of silver
upon the rocks, which slowly rise aloft like water
spirits from the deep, then shiver and break,
and spread, and shroud themselves, and disap-
pear, in a soft mist of foam; nor of the gentle, incessant heaving and panting of the whole
liquid plain; nor of the long waves, keeping
steady time, like a line of soldiery, as they
resounded upon the hollow shore—he would not
deign to notice that restless living element at
all, except to bless his stars that he was not upon
it. Nor the distinct detail, nor the refined coloring, nor the graceful outline and roseate golden
line of the jutting crags, nor the bold shadows
cast from Otus or Laurium by the declining sun
—our agent of a mercantile firm would not
value these matters even at a low figure. Rather
we must turn for the sympathy we seek to yon
pilgrim student, come from a semi-barbarous
land to that small corner of the earth, as to a
shrine, where he might take his fill gazing on
those emblems and coruscations of invisible,
unoriginate perfection. It was the stranger
from a remote province, from Britain or from
Mauritania, who in a scene so different from
that of his chilly, woody swamps, or of his

fiery, choking sands, learned at once what a real university must be, by coming to understand the sort of country which was its suitable home.

Nor was this all that a university required and found in Athens. No one, not even there, could live on poetry. If the students at that famous place had nothing better than bright hues and soothing sounds, they would not have been able or disposed to turn their residence there to much account. Of course they must have the means of living, nay, in a certain sense, of enjoyment, if Athens was to be an *alma mater* at the time, or to remain afterward a pleasant thought in their memory. And so they had: be it recollected Athens was a port and a mart of trade, perhaps the first in Greece; and strangers were ever flocking to it, whose combat was to be with intellectual, not physical difficulties, and who claimed to have their bodily wants supplied that they might be at leisure to set about furnishing their minds.

Now barren as was the soil of Attica, and bare the face of the country, yet it had only too many resources for an elegant, nay, luxurious abode there. So abundant were the imports of the place, that it was a common saying that the productions which were found singly elsewhere were brought together in Athens. Corn and wine, the staple of existence in such a climate, came from the islands of the Ægean; fine wool and carpeting from Asia Minor; slaves, as now, from the Euxine; and timber too, and iron and brass, from the coasts of the Mediterranean. The Athenian did not condescend to manufactures himself, but encouraged them in others, and a population of foreigners caught at the lucrative occupation, both for home consumption and for exportation. Their cloth and other textures for dress and furniture, and their hardware—for instance, armor—were in great request. Labor was cheap; stone and marble in plenty; and the taste and skill, which at first were devoted to public buildings, as temples and porticoes, were in course of time applied to the mansions of public men. If nature did much for Athens, it is undeniable that art did much more.

EDWARD BULWER LYTTON

Born in 1803, died in 1873; educated at Cambridge; member of Parliament in 1831-41, and 1852-66; Colonial Secretary in 1858; raised to the peerage in 1866; his first work, "Falkland," published in 1827; "Last Days of Pompeii" in 1834; besides many other novels, wrote volumes of verse, made translations and wrote dramas, including "The Lady of Lyons" (1838), and "Richelieu" (1839).

THE DESCENT OF VESUVIUS ON POMPEII [1]

On the upper tier (but apart from the male spectators) sat the women, their gay dresses resembling some gaudy flower-bed; it is needless to add that they were the most talkative part of the assembly; and many were the looks directed up to them, especially from the benches appropriated to the young and the unmarried men. On the lower seats round the arena sat the more high-born and wealthy visitors—the magistrates and those of senatorial or equestrian dignity: the passages which, by corridors at the right and left, gave access to these seats, at either end of the oval arena, were also the entrances for the combatants. Strong palings at these passages prevented any unwelcome eccentricity in the movements of the beasts, and con-

[1] From "The Last Days of Pompeii." The great theater at Pompeii, built in the time of Augustus, was semi-circular in form, with a diameter of 322 feet.

fined them to their appointed prey. Around the parapet which was raised above the arena, and from which the seats gradually rose, were gladiatorial inscriptions, and paintings wrought in fresco, typical of the entertainments for which the place was designed. Throughout the whole building wound invisible pipes, from which, as the day advanced, cooling and fragrant showers were to be sprinkled over the spectators.

The officers of the amphitheater were still employed in the task of fixing the vast awning (or *velaria*) which covered the whole, and which luxurious invention the Campanians arrogated to themselves: it was woven of the whitest Apulian wool, and variegated with broad stripes of crimson. Owing either to some inexperience on the part of the workmen or to some defect in the machinery, the awning, however, was not arranged that day so happily as usual; indeed, from the immense space of the circumference, the task was always one of great difficulty and art—so much so that it could seldom be adventured in rough or windy weather. But the present day was so remarkably still that there seemed to the spectators no excuse for the awkwardness of the artificers; and when a large gap in the back of the awning was still visible, from the obstinate refusal of one part of the velaria to ally itself with the rest, the murmurs of discontent were loud and general.

The ædile Pansa,[2] at whose expense the exhibition was given, looked particularly annoyed at

[2] The house of Pansa in Pompeii, as now uncovered, shows one of the largest and most elaborate dwellings in the city. It measures 120 by 300 feet.

the defect, and vowed bitter vengeance on the head of the chief officer of the show, who, fretting, puffing, perspiring, busied himself in idle orders and unavailing threats.

The hubbub ceased suddenly—the operators desisted—the crowd were stilled—the gap was forgotten—for now, with a loud and warlike flourish of trumpets, the gladiators, marshaled in ceremonious procession, entered the arena. They swept round the oval space very slowly and deliberately, in order to give the spectators full leisure to admire their stern serenity of feature—their brawny limbs and various arms, as well as to form such wagers as the excitement of the moment might suggest.

"Oh!" cried the widow Fulvia to the wife of Pansa, as they leaned down from their lofty bench, "do you see that gigantic gladiator? how drolly he is drest!"

"Yes," said the ædile's wife with complacent importance, for she knew all the names and qualities of each combatant: "he is a retiarius or netter; he is armed only, you see, with a three-pronged spear like a trident, and a net; he wears no armor, only the fillet and the tunic. He is a mighty man, and is to fight with Sporus, yon thick-set gladiator, with the round shield and drawn sword but without body armor; he has not his helmet on now, in order that you may see his face—how fearless it is! By-and-by he will fight with his visor down." . . .

While thus conversing, the first formalities of the show were over. To these succeeded a feigned combat with wooden swords between the various gladiators matched against each other.

Among these the skill of two Roman gladiators, hired for the occasion, was the most admired; and next to them the most graceful combatant was Lydon. This sham contest did not last above an hour, nor did it attract any very lively interest except among those connoisseurs of the arena to whom art was preferable to more coarse excitement; the body of the spectators were rejoiced when it was over, and when the sympathy rose to terror. The combatants were now arranged in pairs, as agreed beforehand; their weapons examined; and the grave sports of the day commenced amid the deepest silence—broken only by the exciting and preliminary blast of warlike music.

It was often customary to begin the sports by the most cruel of all; and some bestiarius, or gladiator appointed to the beasts, was slain first as an initiatory sacrifice. But in the present instance the experienced Pansa thought better that the sanguinary drama should advance, not decrease, in interest; and accordingly the execution of Olinthus and Glaucus was reserved for the last. It was arranged that the two horsemen should first occupy the arena; that the foot gladiators, paired off, should then be loosed indiscriminately on the stage; that Glaucus and the lion should next perform their part in the bloody spectacle; and the tiger and the Nazarene be the grand finale. And in the spectacles of Pompeii, the reader of Roman history must limit his imagination, nor expect to find those vast and wholesale exhibitions of magnificent slaughter with which a Nero or a Caligula regaled the inhabitants of the Imperial City. The Roman shows, which absorbed the more celebrated gladiators and the chief proportion of foreign beasts, were indeed the very reason why in the lesser towns of the empire the sports of the amphitheater were comparatively humane and rare; and in this as in other respects, Pompeii was the miniature, the microcosm of Rome. Still, it was an awful and imposing spectacle, with which modern times have, happily, nothing to compare; a vast theater, rising row upon row, and swarming with human beings, from fifteen to eighteen thousand in number, intent upon no fictitious representation—no tragedy of the stage —but the actual victory or defeat, the exultant life or the bloody death, of each and all who entered the arena!

The two horsemen were now at either extremity of the lists (if so they might be called), and at a given signal from Pansa the combatants started simultaneously as in full collision, each advancing his round buckler, each posing on high his sturdy javelin; but just when within three paces of his opponent, the steed of Berbix suddenly halted, wheeled round, and as Nobilior was borne rapidly by, his antagonist spurred upon him. The buckler of Nobilior, quickly and skilfully extended, received a blow which otherwise would have been fatal. And the wild murmur, swelled by many a shout, echoed from side to side.

The visors of both the horsemen were completely closed (like those of the knights in after times), but the head was nevertheless the great point of assault; and Nobilior, now wheeling his charger with no less adroitness than his oppo-

nent, directed his spear full on the helmet of
his foe. Berbix raised his buckler to shield
himself, and his quick-eyed antagonist, suddenly
lowering his weapon, pierced him through the
breast. Berbix reeled and fell.

"Nobilior! Nobilior!" shouted the populace.

"I have lost ten sestertia," said Clodius, between his teeth.

"*Habet!*" (he has it) said Pansa deliberately.

The populace, not yet hardened into cruelty,
made the signal of mercy: but as the attendants
of the arena approached, they found the kindness came too late; the heart of the Gaul had
been pierced, and his eyes were set in death.
It was his life's blood that flowed so darkly
over the sand and sawdust of the arena.

There were now on the arena six combatants:
Niger and his net, matched against Sporus with
his shield and his short broad-sword; Lydon and
Tetraides, naked save by a cincture round the
waist, each armed only with a heavy Greek
cestus; and two gladiators from Rome, clad in
complete steel, and evenly matched with immense bucklers and pointed swords.

The initiatory contest between Lydon and
Tetraides being less deadly than that between
the other combatants, no sooner had they advanced to the middle of the arena than as by
common consent the rest held back, to see how
that contest should be decided, and wait till
fiercer weapons might replace the cestus ere
they themselves commenced hostilities. They
stood leaning on their arms and apart from each
other, gazing on the show, which, if not bloody
enough thoroughly to please the populace, they

were still inclined to admire because its origin was of their ancestral Greece.

No persons could at first glance have seemed less evenly matched than the two antagonists. Tetraides, tho no taller than Lydon, weighed considerably more; the natural size of his muscles was increased, to the eyes of the vulgar, by masses of solid flesh; for, as it was a notion that the contest of the cestus fared easiest with him who was plumpest, Tetraides had encouraged to the utmost his hereditary predisposition to the portly. His shoulders were vast, and his lower limbs thick-set, double-jointed, and slightly curved outward, in that formation which takes so much from beauty to give so largely to strength. But Lydon, except that he was slender even almost to meagerness, was beautifully and delicately proportioned; and the skilful might have perceived that with much less compass of muscle than his foe, that which he had was more seasoned—iron and compact. In proportion, too, as he wanted flesh, he was likely to possess activity; and a haughty smile on his resolute face, which strongly contrasted with the solid heaviness of his enemy's, gave assurance to those who beheld it and united their hope to their pity; so that despite the disparity of their seeming strength, the cry of the multitude was nearly as loud for Lydon as for Tetraides.

Whoever is acquainted with the modern prizering—whoever has witnessed the heavy and disabling strokes which the human fist, skilfully directed, hath the power to bestow—may easily understand how much that happy facility would be increased by a band carried by thongs of leather round the arm as high as the elbow, and terribly strengthened about the knuckles by a plate of iron, and sometimes a plummet of lead. Yet this, which was meant to increase, perhaps rather diminished, the interest of the fray; for it necessarily shortened its duration. A very few blows, successfully and scientifically planted, might suffice to bring the contest to a close; and the battle did not, therefore, often allow full scope for the energy, fortitude, and dogged perseverance that we technically style *pluck*, which not unusually wins the day against superior science, and which heightens to so painful a delight the interest in the battle and the sympathy for the brave.

Tetraides struck—it was as the blow of a smith on a vise; Lydon sank suddenly on one knee—the blow passed over his head. Not so harmless was Lydon's retaliation; he quickly sprang to his feet, and aimed his cestus full on the broad chest of his antagonist. Tetraides reeled—the populace shouted. . . .

The people had been already rendered savage by the exhibition of blood; they thirsted for more; their superstition was aided by their ferocity. Aroused, inflamed by the spectacle of their victims, they forgot the authority of their rulers. It was one of those dread popular convulsions common to crowds wholly ignorant, half free and half servile, and which the peculiar constitution of the Roman provinces so frequently exhibited. The power of the prætor was a reed beneath the whirlwind; still, at his word the guards had drawn themselves along the lower benches, on which the upper classes sat separate from the vulgar. They made but a feeble barrier; the waves of the human sea halted for a moment, to enable Arbacus to count the exact moment of his doom! In despair, and in a terror which beat down even pride, he glanced his eye over the rolling and rushing crowd; when, right above them, through the wide chasm which had been left in the velaria, he beheld a strange and awful apparition; he beheld, and his craft restored his courage!

He stretched his hand on high; over his lofty brow and royal features there came an expression of unutterable solemnity and command.

"Behold!" he roared with a voice of thunder, which stilled the roar of the crowd: "behold how the gods protect the guiltless! The fires of the avenging Orcus burst forth against the false witness of my accusers!"

The eyes of the crowd followed the gesture of the Egyptian, and beheld with dismay a vast vapor shooting from the summit of Vesuvius in the form of a gigantic pine-tree; the trunk, blackness—the breaches fire!—a fire that shifted and wavered in its hues with every moment, now fiercely luminous, now of a dull and dying red, that again blazed terrifically forth with intolerable glare!

There was a dead, heart-sunken silence; through which there suddenly broke the roar of the lion, which was echoed back from within the building by the sharper and fiercer yells of its fellow beasts. Dread seers were they of the Burden of the Atmosphere, and wild prophets of the wrath to come!

Then there arose on high the universal shrieks of women; the men stared at each other, but were dumb. At that moment they felt the earth shake under their feet; the walls of the theater trembled; and beyond in the distance they heard the crash of falling roofs; an instant more, and the mountain cloud seemed to roll toward them, dark and rapid, like a torrent; at the same time it cast forth from its bosom a shower of ashes mixt with vast fragments of burning stone! Over the crushing vines, over the desolate streets, over the amphitheater itself; far and wide, with many a mighty splash in the agitated sea, fell that awful shower!

No longer thought the crowd of justice or of Arbaces; safety for themselves was their sole thought. Each turned to fly—each dashing, pressing, crushing against the other. Trampling recklessly over the fallen, amid groans and oaths and prayers and sudden shrieks, the enormous crowd vomited itself forth through the numerous passages. Whither should they fly? Some, anticipating a second earthquake, hastened to their homes to load themselves with their more costly goods and escape while it was yet time; others, dreading the showers of ashes that now fell fast, torrent upon torrent, over the streets, rushed under the roofs of the nearest houses, or temples, or sheds—shelter of any kind—for protection from the terrors of the open air. But darker, and larger, and mightier, spread the cloud above them. It was a sudden and more ghastly Night rushing upon the realm of Noon!

LORD BEACONSFIELD

Born in 1804, died in 1881; son of Isaac D'Israeli; entered
Parliament in 1837, where he opposed Peel; Chancellor of
Exchequer and leader of the House in 1852, and again in
1858; Chancellor of the Exchequer in 1866; carried the
Reform bill of 1867; Prime Minister in 1868, and again
in 1874-80; made Earl of Beaconsfield in 1876; plenipoten-
tiary at the Congress of Berlin in 1878; published several
novels, including "Vivian Gray" (1826), "Henrietta Temple"
(1837), "Coningsby" (1844), "Sybil" (1845), "Tancred"
(1847), and "Endymion" (1880).

JERUSALEM BY MOONLIGHT [1]

THE broad moon lingers on the summit of
Mount Olivet, but its beam has long left the
garden of Gethsemane and the tomb of Absalom,
the waters of Kedron and the dark abyss of
Jehoshaphat. Full falls its splendor, however,
on the opposite city, vivid and defined in its
silver blaze. A lofty wall, with turrets and
towers, and frequent gates, undulates with the
unequal ground which it covers, as it encircles
the lost capital of Jehovah. It is a city of hills
far more famous than those of Rome: for all
Europe has heard of Zion and of Calvary, while
the Arab and the Assyrian, and the tribes and
nations beyond, are as ignorant of the Capitoline
and Aventine mounts as they are of the Malvern
or the Chiltern hills.

The broad steep of Zion crowned with the

[1] From "Tancred."

31

tower of David; nearer still, Mount Moriah, with the gorgeous temple of the God of Abraham, but, built, alas! by the child of Hagar, and not by Sarah's chosen one; close to its cedars and its cypresses, its lofty spires and airy arches, the moonlight falls upon Bethesda's pool; further on, entered by the gate of St. Stephen, the eye, tho 'tis the noon of night, traces with ease the Street of Grief, a long winding ascent to a vast cupolaed pile that now covers Calvary—called the Street of Grief, because there the most illustrious of the human, as well as of the Hebrew race, the descendant of King David, and the divine son of the most favored of women, twice sank under that burden of suffering and shame which is now throughout all Christendom the emblem of triumph and of honor; passing over groups and masses of houses built of stone, with terraced roofs, or surmounted with small domes, we reach the hill of Salem, where Melchisedek built his mystic citadel; and still remains the hill of Scopas, where Titus gazed upon Jerusalem on the eve of his final assault. Titus destroyed the temple. The religion of Judea has in turn subverted the fanes which were raised to his father and to himself in their imperial capital; and the God of Abraham, of Isaac, and of Jacob is now worshiped before every altar in Rome.

Jerusalem by moonlight! 'Tis a fine spectacle, apart from all its indissoluble associations of awe and beauty. The mitigating hour softens the austerity of a mountain landscape magnificent in outline, however harsh and severe in detail; and, while it retains all its sublimity, removes much of the savage sternness of the strange and unrivaled scene. A fortified city, almost surrounded by ravines, and rising in the center of chains of far-spreading hills, occasionally offering, through their rocky glens, the gleams of a distant and richer land!

The moon has sunk behind the Mount of Olives, and the stars in the darker sky shine doubly bright over the sacred city. The all-prevailing stillness is broken by a breeze, that seems to have traveled over the plain of Sharon from the sea. It wails among the tombs, and sighs among the cypress groves. The palm-tree trembles as it passes, as if it were a spirit of wo. Is it the breeze that has traveled over the plain of Sharon from the sea?

Or is it the haunting voices of prophets mourning over the city that they could not save? Their spirits surely would linger on the land where their Creator had deigned to dwell, and over whose impending fate Omnipotence had shed human tears. From this Mount! Who can but believe that, at the midnight hour, from the summit of the Ascension, the great departed of Israel assembled to gaze upon the battlements of their mystic city! There might be counted heroes and sages, who need shrink from no rivalry with the brightest and the wisest of other lands; but the lawgiver of the time of the Pharaohs, whose laws are still obeyed; the monarch, whose reign has ceased for three thousand years, but whose wisdom is a proverb in all nations of the earth; the teacher, whose doctrines have modeled civilized Europe—the greatest of legislators, the greatest of administrators, and the greatest of reformers—what race, extinct or living, can produce three such men as these!

The last light is extinguished in the village of Bethany. The wailing breeze has become a moaning wind; a white film spreads over the purple sky; the stars are veiled, the stars are hid; all becomes as dark as the waters of Kedron and valley of Jehoshaphat. The tower of David merges into obscurity; no longer glitter the minarets of the mosque of Omar; Bethesda's angelic waters, the gate of Stephen, the street of sacred sorrow, the hill of Salem, and the heights of Scopas can no longer be discerned. Alone in the increasing darkness, while the very line of the walls gradually eludes the eye, the church of the Holy Sepulcher is a beacon-light.

And why is the church of the Holy Sepulcher a beacon-light? Why, when it is already past the noon of darkness, when every soul slumbers in Jerusalem, and not a sound disturbs the deep repose except the howl of the wild dog crying to the wilder wind—why is the cupola of the sanctuary illumined, tho the hour has long since been numbered, when pilgrims there kneel and monks pray?

An armed Turkish guard are bivouacked in the court of the church; within the church itself, two brethren of the convent of Terra Santa keep holy watch and ward; while, at the tomb beneath, there kneels a solitary youth, who prostrated himself at sunset, and who will there pass unmoved the whole of the sacred night.

Yet the pilgrim is not in communion with the Latin Church; neither is he of the Church Armenian, or the Church Greek; Maronite

Coptic, or Abyssinian—these also are Christian churches which can not call him child.

He comes from a distant and a northern isle to bow before the tomb of a descendant of the kings of Israel, because he, in common with all the people of that isle, recognizes in that sublime Hebrew incarnation the presence of a divine Redeemer. Then why does he come alone? It is not that he has availed himself of the inventions of modern science, to repair first to a spot, which all his countrymen may equally desire to visit, and thus anticipate their hurrying arrival. Before the inventions of modern science, all his countrymen used to flock hither. Then why do they not now? Is the Holy Land no longer hallowed? Is it not the land of sacred and mysterious truths? The land of heavenly messages and earthly miracles? The land of prophets and apostles? Is it not the land upon whose mountains the Creator of the Universe parleyed with man, and the flesh of whose anointed race He mystically assumed, when He struck the last blow at the powers of evil? Is it to be believed that there are no peculiar and eternal qualities in a land thus visited, which distinguish it from all others—that Palestine is like Normandy or Yorkshire, or even Attica or Rome?

There may be some who maintain this; there have been some, and those, too, among the wisest and the wittiest of the northern and western races, who, touched by a presumptuous jealousy of the long predominance of that Oriental intellect to which they owed their civilization, would have persuaded themselves and the world that the traditions of Sinai and Calvary were fables. Half a century ago, Europe made a violent and apparently successful effort to disembarrass itself of its Asian faith. The most powerful and the most civilized of its kingdoms, about to conquer the rest, shut up its churches, desecrated its altars, massacred and persecuted their sacred servants, and announced that the Hebrew creeds which Simon Peter brought from Palestine, and which his successors revealed to Clovis, were a mockery and a fiction. What has been the result? In every city, town, village, and hamlet of that great kingdom, the divine image of the most illustrious of Hebrews has been again raised amid the homage of kneeling millions; while, in the heart of its bright and witty capital, the nation has erected the most gorgeous of modern temples, and consecrated its marble and golden walls to the name, and memory, and celestial efficacy of a Hebrew woman.

CHARLES MERIVALE

Born in 1808, died in 1893; educated at Cambridge; became
rector of a parish in 1848; dean of Ely Cathedral in 1869;
published his "History of the Romans Under the Empire"
in 1850-62; "A General History of Rome" in 1875, "Contrast Between Christian and Pagan Society" in 1880.

THE PERSONALITY OF AUGUSTUS
CÆSAR [1]

IN stature Augustus hardly exceeded the
middle height, but his person was lightly and
delicately formed, and its proportions were such
as to convey a favorable and even a striking impression. His countenance was pale, and testi-
fied to the weakness of his health, and almost
constant bodily suffering; but the hardships of
military service had imparted a swarthy tinge
to a complexion naturally fair, and his eyebrows
meeting over a sharp and aquiline nose gave a
serious and stern expression to his countenance.
His hair was light, and his eyes blue and piercing; he was well pleased if any one on approaching him looked on the ground and affected to
be unable to meet their dazzling brightness. It
was said that his dress concealed many imper-

[1] From the "History of the Romans Under the Empire."
Merivale's purpose in writing this book was to fill in the
interval between the unfinished history by Thomas Arnold
and Gibbon.

fections and blemishes on his person; but he could not disguise all the infirmities under which he labored; the weakness of the forefinger of his right hand and a lameness in the left hip were the results of wounds he incurred in a battle with the Iapydæ in early life; he suffered repeated attacks of fever of the most serious kind, especially in the course of the campaign of Philippi and that against the Cantabrians, and again two years afterward at Rome, when his recovery was despaired of. From that time, altho constantly liable to be affected by cold and heat, and obliged to nurse himself throughout with the care of a valetudinarian, he does not appear to have had any return of illness so serious as the preceding; and dying at the age of seventy-four, the rumor obtained popular currency that he was prematurely cut off by poison administered by the empress.

As the natural consequence of this bodily weakness and sickly constitution, Octavian did not attempt to distinguish himself by active exertions or feats of personal prowess. The splendid examples of his uncle the dictator, and of Antonius[2] his rival, might have early discouraged him from attempting to shine as a warrior and hero; he had not the vivacity and animal spirits necessary to carry him through such exploits as theirs; and, altho he did not shrink from exposing himself to personal danger, he prudently declined to allow a comparison to to be instituted between himself and rivals whom he could not hope to equal. Thus necessarily thrown back upon other resources, he trusted to

[2] Mark Antony.

caution and circumspection, first to preserve his own life, and afterward to obtain the splendid prizes which had hitherto been carried off by daring adventure, and the good fortune which is so often its attendant. His contest therefore with Antonius and Sextus Pompeius was the contest of cunning with bravery; but from his youth upward he was accustomed to overreach, not the bold and reckless only, but the most considerate and wily of his contemporaries, such as Cicero and Cleopatra; he succeeded in the end in deluding the senate and people of Rome in the establishment of his tyranny; and finally deceived the expectations of the world, and falsified the lessons of the republican history, in reigning himself forty years in disguise, and leaving a throne to be claimed without challenge by his successors for fourteen centuries.

But altho emperor in name, and in fact absolute master of his people, the manners of the Cæsar, both in public and private life, were still those of a simple citizen. On the most solemn occasions he was distinguished by no other dress than the robes and insignia of the offices which he exercised; he was attended by no other guards than those which his consular dignity rendered customary and decent. In his court there was none of the etiquette of modern monarchies to be recognized, and it was only by slow and gradual encroachment that it came to prevail in that of his successors. Augustus was contented to take up his residence in the house which had belonged to the orator Licinius Calvus, in the neighborhood of the Forum; which he afterward abandoned for that of Hortensius on the Palatine, of which Suetonius observes that it was remarkable neither for size nor splendor. Its halls were small, and lined, not with marble, after the luxurious fashion of many patrician palaces, but with the common Alban stone, and the pattern of the pavement was plain and simple. Nor when he succeeded Lepidus in the pontificate would he relinquish this private dwelling for the regia or public residence assigned that honorable office.

Many anecdotes are recorded of the moderation with which the emperor received the opposition, and often the rebukes, of individuals in public as well as in private. These stories are not without their importance, as showing how little formality there was in the tone of addressing the master of the Roman world, and how entirely different were the ideas of the nation were, with regard to the position occupied by the Cæsar and his family from those with which modern associations have imbued us. We have already noticed the rude freedom with which Tiberius was attacked, altho step-son of the emperor, and participating in the eminent functions of the tribunitian power, by a declaimer in the schools at Rhodes: but Augustus himself seems to have suffered almost as much as any private citizen from the general coarseness of behavior which characterized the Romans in their public assemblies, and the rebukes to which he patiently submitted were frequently such as would lay the courtier of a constitutional sovereign in modern Europe under perpetual disgrace.

On one occasion, for instance, in the public

discharge of his functions as corrector of manners, he had brought a specific charge against a certain knight for having squandered his patrimony. The accused proved that he had, on the contrary, augmented it. "Well," answered the emperor, somewhat annoyed by his error, "but you are at all events living in celibacy, contrary to recent enactments." The other was able to reply that he was married, and was the father of three legitimate children; and when the emperor signified that he had no further charges to bring, added aloud: "Another time, Cæsar, when you give ear to informations against honest men, take care that your informants are honest themselves." Augustus felt the justice of the rebuke thus publicly administered, and submitted to it in silence.

ALEXANDER W. KINGLAKE

Born in 1809, died in 1891; traveled in the East and published "Eothen; or Traces of Travel Brought Home from the East," in 1844; visited Algiers in 1845; went with the British army to the Crimea in 1854, remaining until the siege of Sebastopol; a member of Parliament in 1857-68; published his "Invasion of the Crimea" in 1863-87.

I

ON MOCKING AT THE SPHINX[1]

AND near the Pyramids, more wondrous and more awful than all else in the land of Egypt, there sits the lonely Sphinx. Comely the creature is, but the comeliness is not of this world; the once worshiped beast is a deformity and a monster to this generation, and yet you can see that those lips, so thick and heavy, were fashioned according to some ancient mold of beauty—some mold of beauty now forgotten—forgotten because that Greece drew forth Cytherea from the flashing foam of the Ægean, and in her image created new forms of beauty, and made it a law among men that the short and proudly wreathed lip should stand for the sign and the main condition of loveliness through all generations to come. Yet still there lives on the race of those who were beautiful in the fashion of the elder world, and Christian girls of Coptic blood will look on

[1] From "Eothen," which long since took its place as a classic among books of travel.

42

you with the sad, serious gaze, and kiss your charitable hand with the big pouting lips of the very Sphinx.

Laugh and mock if you will at the worship of stone idols; but mark ye this, ye breakers of images, that in one regard the stone idol bears awful semblance of Deity—unchangefulness in the midst of changes—the same seeming will and intent for ever and ever inexorable! Upon ancient dynasties of Ethiopian and Egyptian kings—upon Greek and Roman, upon Arab and Ottoman conquerors—upon Napoleon dreaming of an Eastern empire—upon battle and pestilence —upon the ceaseless misery of the Egyptian race —upon keen-eyed travelers—Herodotus yesterday, and Warburton to-day—upon all and more this unworldly Sphinx has watched, and watched like a Providence with the same earnest eyes, and the same sad, tranquil mien. And we, we shall die, and Islam will wither away, and the Englishman straining far over to hold his loved India, will plant a firm foot on the banks of the Nile, and sit in the seats of the Faithful, and still that sleepless rock will lie watching and watching the works of the new busy race, with those same sad earnest eyes, and the same tranquil mien everlasting. You dare not mock at the Sphinx!

II

THE BEGINNING OF THE CRIMEAN
WAR [2]

LOOKING back upon the troubles which ended
in the outbreak of war, one sees the nations at
first swaying backward and forward like a throng
so vast as to be helpless, but afterward falling
slowly into warlike array. And when one begins to search for the man or the men whose
volition was governing the crowd, the eye falls
upon the towering form of the Emperor Nicholas.
He was not single-minded, and therefore his will
was unstable, but it had a huge force; and, since
he was armed with the whole authority of his
empire, it seemed plain that it was this man
—and only he—who was bringing danger from
the north. And at first, too, it seemed that
within his range of action there was none who
could be his equal: but in a little while the looks
of men were turned to the Bosporus, for thither
his ancient adversary was slowly bending his
way.

To fit him for the encounter, the Englishman
was clothed with little authority except what he
could draw from the resources of his own mind
and from the strength of his own wilful nature.

[2] From "The Invasion of the Crimea," one of the master-
pieces of modern historical literature, but often criticized
for its excessive bias against France as represented by
Napoleon III.

Yet it was presently seen that those who were near him fell under his dominion, and did as he bid them, and that the circle of deference to his will was always increasing around him; and soon it appeared that, tho he moved gently, he began to have mastery over a foe who was consuming his strength in mere anger. When he had conquered, he stood, as it were, with folded arms, and seemed willing to desist from strife. But also in the west there had been seen a knot of men possest for the time of the mighty engine of the French State, and striving so to use it as to be able to keep their hold, and to shelter themselves from a cruel fate. The volitions of these men were active enough, because they were toiling for their lives. Their efforts seemed to interest and to please the lustiest man of those days, for he watched them from over the Channel with approving smile, and began to declare, in his good-humored, boisterous way, that so long as they should be suffered to have the handling of France, *so long as they would execute for him his policy*, so long as they would take care not to deceive him, they ought to be encouraged, they ought to be made use of, they ought to have the shelter they wanted; and, the Frenchmen agreeing to his conditions, he was willing to level the barrier—he called it perhaps false pride—which divided the government of the Queen from the venturers of the 2d of December. In this thought, at the moment, he stood almost alone; but he abided his time. At length he saw the spring of 1853, bringing with it grave peril to the Ottoman State. Then, throwing aside with a laugh some papers which belonged to the Home

Office, he gave his strong shoulder to the leveling work. Under the weight of his touch the barrier fell. Thenceforth the hindrances that met him were but slight. As he from the first had willed it, so moved the two great nations of the West.

CHARLES DARWIN

Born in 1809, died in 1882; grandson of Erasmus Darwin; educated at Edinburgh and Cambridge; went around the world on a scientific expedition in 1831-36; settled in Kent in 1842 and thenceforth devoted his life to scientific research; published "The Origin of Species" in 1859, "The Descent of Man" in 1871, "The Emotions of Man and Animals" in 1872.

I

ON VARIATIONS IN MAMMALS, BIRDS AND FISHES[1]

NOT only the various domestic races, but the most distinct genera and orders within the same great class—for instance, mammals, birds, reptiles, and fishes—are all the descendants of one common progenitor, and we must admit that the whole vast amount of difference between these forms has primarily arisen from simple variability. To consider the subject under this point of view is enough to strike one dumb with amazement. But our amazement ought to be lessened when we reflect that beings almost infinite in number, during an almost infinite lapse of time, have often had their whole organization rendered in some degree plastic, and that each slight modification of structure which was in any way beneficial under excessively complex conditions of life has been preserved, while each which was in any

[1] From "The Origin of Species."

47

way injurious has been rigorously destroyed. And the long-continued accumulation of beneficial variations will infallibly have led to structures as diversified, as beautifully adapted for various purposes, and as excellently coordinated as we see in the animals and plants around us. Hence I have spoken of selection as the paramount power, whether applied by man to the formation of domestic breeds, or by nature to the production of species. If an architect were to rear a noble and commodious edifice without the use of cut stone, by selecting from the fragments at the base of a precipice wedge-formed stones for his arches, elongated stones for his lintels, and flat stones for his roof, we should admire his skill, and regard him as the paramount power. Now, the fragments of stone, tho indispensable to the architect, bear to the edifice built by him the same relation which the fluctuating variations of organic beings bear to the varied and admirable structures ultimately acquired by their modified descendants.

Some authors have declared that natural selection explains nothing, unless the precise cause of each slight individual difference be made clear. If it were explained to a savage utterly ignorant of the art of building how the edifice had been raised stone upon stone, and why wedge-formed fragments were used for the arches, flat stones for the roof, etc.; and if the use of each part and of the whole building were pointed out, it would be unreasonable if he declared that nothing had been made clear to him, because the precise cause of the shape of each fragment could not be told. But this is a nearly parallel case with the objection that selection explains nothing, because we know not the cause of each individual difference in the structure of each being.

The shape of the fragments of stone at the base of our precipice may be called accidental, but this is not strictly correct; for the shape of each depends on a long sequence of events, all obeying natural laws; on the nature of the rock, on the lines of deposition or cleavage, on the form of the mountain, which depends on its upheaval and subsequent denudation, and lastly on the storm or earthquake which throws down the fragments. But in regard to the use to which the fragments may be put, their shape may be strictly said to be accidental. And here we are led to face a great difficulty, in alluding to which I am aware I am traveling beyond my proper province. An omniscient Creator must have foreseen every consequence which results from the laws imposed by Him.

But can it reasonably be maintained that the Creator intentionally ordered, if we use the words in any ordinary sense, that certain fragments of rock should assume certain shapes so that the builder might erect his edifice? If the various laws which have determined the shape of each fragment were not predetermined for the builder's sake, can it be maintained with any greater probability that He specially ordained for the sake of the breeder each of the innumerable variations in our domestic animals and plants; many of these variations being of no service to man, and not beneficial, far more often injurious, to the creatures themselves? Did he ordain that the crop and tail-feathers of the pigeon should vary in order that the fancier might make his grotesque pouter and fantail breeds? Did He cause the frame and mental qualities of the dog to vary in order that a breed might be formed of indomitable ferocity, with jaws fitted to pin down the bull for man's brutal sport? But if we give up the principle in one case—if we do not admit that the variations of the primeval dog were intentionally guided in order that the greyhound, for instance, that perfect image of symmetry and vigor, might be formed—no shadow of reason can be assigned for the belief that variations, alike in nature and the result of the same general laws, which have been the ground-work through natural selection of the formation of the most perfectly adapted animals in the world, man included, were intentionally and specially guided. However much we may wish it, we can hardly follow Professor Asa Gray in his belief, "that variation has been led along certain beneficial lines of irrigation." If we assume that each particular variation was from the beginning of all time preordained, then that plasticity of organization which leads to many injurious deviations of structure, as well as the redundant power of reproduction which inevitably leads to a struggle for existence, and as a consequence, to the natural selection or survival of the fittest, must appear to us superfluous laws of nature. On the other hand, an omnipotent and omniscient Creator ordains everything and foresees everything. Thus we are brought face to face with a difficulty as insoluble as is that of free will and predestination.

II

THE GENESIS OF A GREAT BOOK [2]

DURING the voyage of the *Beagle* I had been deeply imprest by discovering in the Pampean formation great fossil animals, covered with armor like that on the existing armadillos; secondly, by the manner in which closely allied animals replace one another in proceeding southward over the Continent; and thirdly, by the South American character of most of the productions of the Galapagos Archipelago, and more especially by the manner in which they differ slightly on each island of the group; none of the islands appearing to be very ancient in a geological sense.

It was evident that such facts as these, as well as many others, could only be explained on the supposition that species gradually become modified; and the subject haunted me. But it was equally evident that neither the action of the surrounding conditions, nor the will of the organisms (especially in the case of plants), could account for the innumerable cases in which organisms of every kind are beautifully adapted to their habits of life; for instance, a woodpecker or a tree-frog to climb trees, or a seed for dispersal by hooks or plumes. I had always been much struck by such adaptations, and until these

[2] From Darwin's "Autobiography," as printed in Volume I of the "Life and Letters." Published by D. Appleton & Co.

could be explained it seemed to me almost useless to endeavor to prove by indirect evidence that species have been modified.

After my return to England it appeared to me that by following the example of Lyell in geology, and by collecting all facts which bore in any way on the variation of animals and plants under domestication and nature, some light might perhaps be thrown on the whole subject. My first notebook was opened in July, 1837. I worked on true Baconian principles; and without any theory collected facts on a wholesale scale, more especially with respect to domesticated productions, by printed inquiries, by conversation with skilful breeders and gardeners, and by extensive reading. When I see the list of books of all kinds which I read and abstracted, including whole series of Journals and Transactions, I am surprized at my industry. I soon perceived that selection was the keystone of man's success in making useful races of animals and plants. But how selection could be applied to organisms living in a state of nature, remained for some time a mystery to me.

In October, 1838—that is, fifteen months after I had begun my systematic inquiry—I happened to read for amusement "Malthus on Population"; and being well prepared to appreciate the struggle for existence which everywhere goes on from long-continued observation of the habits of animals and plants, it at once struck me that under these circumstances favorable variations would tend to be preserved, and unfavorable ones to be destroyed. The result of this would be the formation of new species. Here then I had at last got a theory by which to work; but I was so anxious to avoid prejudice that I determined not for some time to write even the briefest sketch of it. In June, 1842, I first allowed myself the satisfaction of writing a very brief abstract of my theory in pencil in thirty-five pages; and this was enlarged during the summer of 1844 into one of two hundred and thirty pages, which I had fairly copied out and still possess.

But at that time I overlooked one problem of great importance; and it is astonishing to me, except on the principle of Columbus and his egg, how I could have overlooked it and its solution. This problem is the tendency in organic beings descended from the same stock to diverge in character as they become modified. That they have diverged greatly is obvious from the manner in which species of all kinds can be classed under genera, genera under families, families under suborders, and so forth: and I can remember the very spot in the road, while in my carriage, when to my joy the solution occurred to me; and this was long after I had come to Down. The solution, as I believe, is that the modified offspring of all dominant and increasing forms tend to become adapted to many and highly diversified places in the economy of nature.

Early in 1856 Lyell advised me to write out my views pretty fully, and I began at once to do so on a scale three or four times as extensive as that which was afterward followed in my "Origin of Species"; yet it was only an abstract of the materials which I had collected, and I got through about half the work on this scale. But my plans were overthrown, for early in the summer of 1858 Mr. Wallace, who was then in the Malay Archipelago, sent me an essay "On the Tendency of Varieties to Depart Indefinitely from the Original Type"; and this essay contained exactly the same theory as mine. Mr. Wallace exprest the wish that if I thought well of his essay, I should send it to Lyell for perusal.

The circumstances under which I consented, at the request of Lyell and Hooker, to allow of an abstract from my MS., together with a letter to Asa Gray dated September 5th, 1857, to be published at the same time with Wallace's essay, are given in the "Journal of the Proceedings of the Linnean Society," 1858, page 45. I was at first very unwilling to consent, as I thought Mr. Wallace might consider my doing so unjustifiable, for I did not then know how generous and noble was his disposition. The extract from my MS. and the letter to Asa Gray had neither been intended for publication, and were badly written. Mr. Wallace's essay, on the other hand, was admirabl: exprest and quite clear. Nevertheless, our joint productions excited very little attention, and the only published notice of them which I can remember was by Professor Haughton of Dublin, whose verdict was that all that was new in them was false, and what was true was old. This shows how necessary it is that any new view should be explained at considerable length in order to arouse public attention. . . .

My habits are methodical, and this has been of not a little use for my particular line of work. Lastly, I have had ample leisure from not having to earn my own bread. Even ill health, tho it has annihilated several years of my life, has saved me from the distractions of society and amusement.

Therefore my success as a man of science, whatever this may have amounted to, has been determined as far as I can judge by complex and diversified mental qualities and conditions. Of these, the most important have been the love of science, unbounded patience in long reflecting over any subject, industry in observing and collecting facts, and a fair share of invention as well as of common sense. With such moderate abilities as I possess, it is truly surprizing that I should have influenced to a considerable extent the belief of scientific men on some important points.

JOHN BROWN

Born in 1810, died in 1882; son of a Biblical scholar of the same name; studied medicine at Edinburgh University and practised medicine successfully in Edinburgh until his death; published the first volume of the "Horæ Subsecivæ" in 1858, the second in 1861, and the third in 1882; one of these contained his best known work, "Rab and His Friends," frequently printed separately since his death.

RAB AND THE GAME CHICKEN[1]

FOUR-AND-THIRTY years ago Bob Ainslie and I were coming up Infirmary Street from the Edinburgh High School, our heads together, and our arms intertwisted, as only lovers and boys know how, or why.

When we got to the top of the street, and turned north, we espied a crowd at the Tron Church. "A dog fight!" shouted Bob, and was off; and so was I, both of us all but praying that it might not be over before we got up! And is not this boy-nature? and human nature too? and don't we all wish a house on fire not to be out before we see it? Dogs like fighting; old Isaac says they "delight" in it, and for the best of all reasons; and boys are not cruel because they like to see the fight. They see three of the great cardinal virtues of dog or man—courage, endurance, and skill—in intense action. This is very different from a love of making dogs fight, and enjoying, and aggravating, and making gain

[1] From "Rab and His Friends."

by their pluck. A boy, be he ever so fond himself of fighting, if he be a good boy, hates and despises all this, but he would have run off with Bob and me fast enough; it is a natural, and a not wicked interest, that all boys and men have in witnessing intense energy in action.

Does any curious and finely ignorant woman wish to know how Bob's eye at a glance announced a dog fight to his brain? He did not, he could not see the dogs fighting; it was a flash of an inference, a rapid induction. The crowd round a couple of dogs fighting is a crowd masculine mainly, with an occasional active, compassionate woman, fluttering wildly round the outside, and using her tongue and her hands freely upon the men, as so many "brutes"; it is a crowd annular, compact, and mobile; a crowd centripetal, having its eyes and its heads all bent downward and inward to one common focus.

Well, Bob and I are up, and find it is not over; a small, thoroughbred, white bull-terrier is busy throttling a large shepherd's dog, unaccustomed to war, but not to be trifled with. They are hard at it; the scientific little fellow doing his work in great style, his pastoral enemy fighting wildly, but with the sharpest of teeth and a great courage. Science and breeding, however, soon had their own; the Game Chicken, as the premature Bob called him, working his way up, took his final grip of poor Yarrow's throat—and he lay gasping and done for. His master, a brown, handsome, big young shepherd from Tweedsmuir, would have liked to have knocked down any man, would "drink up Esil, or eat a crocodile," for that part, if he had a chance: it was no use kicking the little dog; that would only make him hold the closer. Many were the means shouted out in mouthfuls, of the best possible ways of ending it. "Water!" but there was none near, and many cried for it who might have got it from the well at Blackfriars Wynd. "Bite the tail!" and a large, vague, benevolent, middle-aged man, more desirous than wise, with some struggle got the bushy end of Yarrow's tail into his ample mouth, and bit it with all his might. This was more than enough for the much-enduring, much-perspiring shepherd, who, with a gleam of joy over his broad visage, delivered a terrific facer upon our large, benevolent, middle-aged friend— who went down like a shot.

Still the Chicken holds; death not far off. "Snuff! a pinch of snuff!" observed a calm, highly-drest young buck, with an eyeglass in his eye. "Snuff, indeed!" growled the angry crowd, affronted and glaring. "Snuff! a pinch of snuff!" again observes the buck, but with more urgency; whereon were produced several open boxes, and from a mull which may have been at Culloden, he took a pinch, knelt down, and presented it to the nose of the Chicken. The laws of physiology and of snuff take their course; the Chicken sneezes, and Yarrow is free!

The young pastoral giant stalks off with Yarrow in his arms—comforting him.

But the bull terrier's blood is up, and his soul unsatisfied; he grips the first dog he meets, and discovering she is not a dog, in Homeric phrase, he makes a brief sort of *amende*, and is off. The boys, with Bob and me at their head, are after him: down Niddry Street he goes bent on mischief; up the Cowgate like an arrow—Bob and I, and our small men panting behind.

There, under the single arch of the South Bridge, is a huge mastiff, sauntering down the middle of the causeway, as if with his hands in his pockets; he is old, gray, brindled, as big as a little Highland bull, and has the Shakespearean dewlaps shaking as he goes.

The Chicken makes straight at him and fastens on his throat. To our astonishment, the great creature does nothing but stand still, hold himself up and roar—yes, roar; a long, serious, remonstrative roar. How is this? Bob and I are up to them. *He is muzzled!* The bailies had proclaimed a general muzzling, and his master, studying strength and economy mainly, had encompassed his huge jaws in a home-made apparatus constructed out of the leather of some ancient *breechin.* His mouth was open as far as it could be; his lips curled up in rage—a sort of terrible grin; his teeth gleaming, ready, from out the darkness; the strap across his mouth tense as a bowstring; his whole frame stiff with indignation and surprize; his roar asking us all round, "Did you ever see the like of this?" He looked a statue of anger and astonishment done in Aberdeen granite.

We soon had a crowd; the Chicken held on. "A knife!" cried Bob; and a cobbler gave him his knife: you know the kind of knife, worn away obliquely to a point, and always keen. I put its edge to the tense leather; it ran before it; and then!—one sudden jerk of that enormous head, a sort of dirty mist about his mouth, no noise—and the bright and fierce little fellow is dropt, limp and dead. A solemn pause; this was more than any of us had bargained for. I turned the little fellow over, and saw he was quite dead; the mastiff had taken him by the small of the back like a rat, and broken it.

He looked down at his victim appeased, ashamed, and amazed; snuffed him all over, stared at him, and taking a sudden thought, turned round and trotted off. Bob took the dead dog up and said, "John, we'll bury him after tea." "Yes," said I, and was off after the mastiff. He made up the Cowgate at rapid swing; he had forgotten some engagement. He turned up the Candlemaker Row, and stopt at the Harrow Inn.

There was a carrier's cart ready to start, and a keen, thin, impatient, black-a-vised little man, his hand at his gray horse's head, looking about angrily for something.

"Rab, ye thief!" said he, aiming a kick at my great friend, who drew cringing up, and avoiding the heavy shoe with more agility than dignity, and, watching his master's eye, slunk dismayed under the cart—his ears down, and as much as he had of tail down too.

What a man this must be—thought I—to whom my tremendous hero turns tail! The carrier saw the muzzle hanging, cut and useless, from his neck, and I eagerly told him the story, which Bob and I always thought, and still think, Homer or King David or Sir Walter alone were worthy to rehearse. The severe little man was mitigated, and condescended to say, "Rab, my man, puir Rabbie"—whereupon the stump of a tail rose up, the ears were cocked, the eyes filled, and were comforted; the two friends were reconciled. "Hupp!" and a stroke of the whip were given to Jess; and off went the three.

Bob and I buried the Game Chicken that night (we had not much of a tea) in the back green of his house in Melville Street, No. 17, with considerable gravity and silence; and being at the time in the "Iliad," and, like all boys, Trojans, we called him Hector, of course.

WILLIAM M. THACKERAY

Born in 1811, died in 1863; lived in India until five years
old; educated at Cambridge; began to write for newspapers
in 1833; went to Paris to study art in 1834; visited the
East in 1844, and the United States in 1852 and 1854;
published "Vanity Fair" in 1846-48, "Pendennis" in
1848-50, "Henry Esmond" in 1852, "The Newcomes" in
1853-55, "The Virginians" in 1857-59.

I

THE IMPERTURBABLE MARLBOROUGH[1]

AND now, having seen a great military march
through a friendly country, the pomps and fes-
tivities of more than one German court, the
severe struggle of a hotly contested battle, and
the triumph of victory, Mr. Esmond beheld
another part of military duty; our troops entering the enemy's territory and putting all around
them to fire and sword; burning farms, wasted
fields, shrieking women, slaughtered sons and
fathers, and drunken soldiery, cursing and carous-
ing in the midst of tears, terror, and murder.
Why does the stately Muse of History, that de-
lights in describing the valor of heroes and the
grandeur of conquest, leave out these scenes,
so brutal, and degrading, that yet form by far
the greater part of the drama of war? You
gentlemen of England, who live at home at ease
and compliment yourselves in the songs of

[1] From "The History of Henry Esmond."

triumph with which our chieftains are bepraised;
you pretty maidens that come tumbling down the
stairs when the fife and drum call you, and
huzza for the British Grenadiers,—do you take
account that these items go to make up the
amount of triumph you admire, and form part
of the duties of the heroes you fondle?

Our chief, whom England and all Europe, sav-
ing only the Frenchmen, worshipt almost, had
this of the god-like in him: that he was impassible
before victory, before danger, before defeat. Before the greatest obstacle or the most trivial
ceremony; before a hundred thousand men drawn
in battalia, or a peasant slaughtered at the door
of his burning hovel; before a carouse of drunken
German lords, or a monarch's court, or a cottage
table where his plans were laid, or an enemy's
battery, vomiting flame and death and strewing
corpses round about him,—he was always cold,
calm, resolute, like fate. He performed a treason
or a court bow, he told a falsehood as black as
Styx, as easily as he paid a compliment or
spoke about the weather. He took a mistress and
left her, he betrayed his benefactor and supported him, or would have murdered him, with the
same calmness always and having no more remorse than Clotho when she weaves the thread,
or Lachesis when she cuts it. In the hour of
battle I have heard the Prince of Savoy's officers
say the prince became possest with a sort of
warlike fury: his eyes lighted up; he rushed
hither and thither, raging; shrieked curses and
encouragement, yelling and harking his bloody
war-dogs on, and himself always at the first of
the hunt. Our duke was as calm at the mouth of

a cannon as at the door of a drawing-room. Perhaps he could not have been the great man he was had he had a heart either for love or hatred, or pity or fear, or regret or remorse. He achieved the highest deed or daring, or deepest calculation of thought, as he performed the very meanest action of which a man is capable; told a lie or cheated a fond woman or robbed a poor beggar of a halfpenny, with a like awful serenity, and equal capacity of the highest and lowest acts of our nature.

His qualities were pretty well known in the army, where there were parties of all politics, and of plenty of shrewdness and wit; but there existed such a perfect confidence in him, as the first captain of the world, and such a faith and admiration in his prodigious genius and fortune, that the very men whom he notoriously cheated of their pay, the chiefs whom he used and injured—for he used all men, great and small, that came near him, as his instruments alike, and took something of theirs, either some quality or some property: the blood of a soldier, it might be, or a jeweled hat or a hundred thousand crowns from the king, or a portion out of a starving sentinel's three farthings; or when he was young, a kiss from a woman, and the gold chain off her neck, taking all he could from woman or man, and having, as I said, this of the godlike in him, that he could see a hero perish or a sparrow fall with the same amount of sympathy for either.

Not that he had no tears, he could always order up this reserve at the proper moment to battle; he could draw upon tears or smiles alike, and whenever need was for using this cheap coin. He would cringe to a shoeblack, and he would flatter a minister or a monarch; be haughty, be humble, threaten, repent, weep, grasp your hand, or stab you whenever he saw occasion —but yet those of the army who knew him best and had suffered most from him, admired him most of all; and as he rode along the lines to battle, or galloped up in the nick of time to a battalion reeling from the enemy's charge or shot, the fainting men and officers got new courage as they saw the splendid calm of his face, and felt that his will made them irresistible.

After the great victory of Blenheim, the enthusiasm of the army for the duke, even of his bitterest personal enemies in it, amounted to a sort of rage: nay, the very officers who cursed him in their hearts were among the most frantic to cheer him. Who could refuse his meed of admiration to such a victory and such a victor? Not he who writes: a man may profess to be ever so much a philosopher, but he who fought on that day must feel a thrill of pride as he recalls it.

II

AT THE BALL BEFORE THE BATTLE OF WATERLOO [2]

THERE never was, since the days of Darius, such a brilliant train of camp-followers as hung round the train of the Duke of Wellington's

[2] From "Vanity Fair."

army in the Low Countries, in 1815, and led it dancing and feasting, as it were, up to the very brink of battle. A certain ball[3] which a noble duchess gave at Brussels on the 15th of June in the above-named year is historical. All Brussels had been in a state of excitement about it; and I have heard from ladies who were in that town at the period, that the talk and interest of persons of their own sex regarding the ball was much greater even than in respect of the enemy in their front. The struggles, intrigues, and prayers to get tickets were such as only English ladies will employ, in order to gain admission to the society of the great of their own nation.

Jos and Mrs. O'Dowd, who were panting to be asked, strove in vain to procure tickets; but others of our friends were more lucky. For instance, through the interest of my Lord Bareacres, and as a set-off for the dinner at the restaurateur's, George got a card for Captain and Mrs. Osborne; which circumstance greatly elated him. Dobbin, who was a friend of the general commanding the division in which their regiment was, came laughing one day to Mrs. Osborne, and displayed a similar invitation; which made Jos envious, and George wonder how the deuce *he* should be getting into society. Mr. and Mrs. Rawdon, finally, were of course invited, as became the friends of a general commanding a cavalry brigade.

On the appointed night, George, having commanded new dresses and ornaments of all sorts for Amelia, drove to the famous ball, where his

[3] Readers will recall Byron's account of this ball in "Childe Harold."

wife did not know a single soul. After looking about for Lady Bareacres,—who cut him, thinking the card was quite enough,—and after placing Amelia on a bench, he left her to her own cogitations there; thinking on his own part that he had behaved very handsomely in getting her new clothes, and bringing her to the ball, where she was free to amuse herself as she liked. Her thoughts were not the pleasantest, and nobody except honest Dobbin came to disturb them.

Whilst her appearance was an utter failure (as her husband felt with a sort of rage), Mrs. Rawdon Crawley's *début* was, on the contrary, very brilliant. She arrived very late. Her face was radiant; her dress perfection. In the midst of the great persons assembled, and the eyeglasses directed to her, Rebecca seemed to be as cool and collected as when she used to marshal Miss Pinkerton's little girls to church. Numbers of the men she knew already, and the dandies thronged around her. As for the ladies, it was whispered among them that Rawdon had run away with her from out of a convent, and that she was a relation of the Montmorency family. She spoke French so perfectly that there might be some truth in this report, and it was agreed that her manners were fine, and her air *distinguished*. Fifty would-be partners thronged round her at once, and prest to have the honor to dance with her. But she said she was engaged, and only going to dance very little; and made her way at once to the place where Emmy sate quite unnoticed, and dismally unhappy.

And so, to finish the poor child at once, Mrs. Rawdon ran and greeted affectionately her dearest Amelia, and began forthwith to patronize her. She found fault with her friend's dress, and her hair-dresser, and wondered how she could be so *chaussée*, and vowed that she must send her *corsetière* the next morning. She vowed that it was a delightful ball; that there was everybody that every one knew, and only a *very* few nobodies in the whole room. It is a fact that in a fortnight, and after three dinners in general society, this young woman had got up the genteel jargon so well that a native could not speak it better; and it was only from her French being so good, that you could know that she was not a born woman of fashion.

George, who had left Emmy on the bench on entering the ballroom, very soon found his way back when Rebecca was by her dear friend's side. Becky was just lecturing Mrs. Osborne upon the follies which her husband was committing. "For God's sake, stop him from gambling, my dear," she said, "or he will ruin himself. He and Rawdon are playing at cards every night; and you know he is very poor, and Rawdon will win every shilling from him if he does not take care. Why don't you prevent him, you little careless creature? Why don't you come to us of an evening, instead of moping at home with that Captain Dobbin? I dare say he is *très aimable;* but how can one love a man with feet of such size? Your husband's feet are darlings—here he comes. Where have you been, wretch? Here is Emmy crying her eyes out for you. Are you coming to fetch me for the quadrille?" And she left her bouquet and shawl by Amelia's side, and tript off with George to dance. Women only know how to wound so. There is a poison on the tip of the little shafts which sting a thousand times more than a man's blunter weapon. Our poor Emmy, who had never hated, never sneered all her life, was powerless in the hands of her remorseless little enemy.

George danced with Rebecca twice or thrice—how many times Amelia scarcely knew. She sat quite unnoticed in her corner, except when Rawdon came up with some words of clumsy conversation; and later in the evening, when Captain Dobbin made so bold as to bring her refreshments and sit beside her. He did not like to ask her why she was so sad; but as a pretext for the tears which were filling her eyes, she told him that Mrs. Crawley had alarmed her by telling her that George would go on playing.

"It is curious, when a man is bent upon play, by what clumsy rogues he will allow himself to be cheated," Dobbin said; and Emmy said "Indeed." She was thinking of something else. It was not the loss of the money that grieved her.

At last George came back for Rebecca's shawl and flowers. She was going away. She did not even condescend to come back and say good-by to Amelia. The poor girl let her husband come and go without saying a word, and her head fell on her breast. Dobbin had been called away, and was whispering deep in conversation with the general of the division, his friend, and had not seen this last parting. George went away then with the bouquet; but when he gave it to the owner, there lay a note, coiled like a snake among the flowers. Rebecca's eye caught it at

69

once: she had been used to deal with notes in early life. She put out her hand and took the nosegay. He saw by her eyes as they met, that she was aware what she would find there. Her husband hurried her away, still too intent upon his own thoughts, seemingly, to take note of any marks of recognition which might pass between his friend and his wife. These were, however, but trifling. Rebecca gave George her hand with one of her usual quick knowing glances, and made a curtsey and walked away. George bowed over the hand; said nothing in reply to a remark of Crawley's,—did not hear it even, his brain was so throbbing with triumph and excitement; and allowed them to go away without a word.

His wife saw the one part at least of the bouquet scene. It was quite natural that George should come at Rebecca's request to get her scarf and flowers,—it was no more than he had done twenty times before in the course of the last few days; but now it was too much for her. "William," she said, suddenly clinging to Dobbin, who was near her, "you've always been very kind to me: I'm—I'm not well. Take me home." She did not know she called him by his Christian name, as George was accustomed to do. He went away with her quickly. Her lodgings were hard by; and they threaded through the crowd without, where everything seemed to be more astir than even in the ballroom within.

George had been angry twice or thrice at finding his wife up on his return from the parties which he frequented, so she went straight to bed now; but altho she did not sleep, and altho

the din and clatter and the galloping of horsemen was incessant, she never heard any of these
noises, having quite other disturbances to keep
her awake.

Osborne meanwhile, wild with elation, went off
to a play table and began to bet frantically. He
won repeatedly. "Everything succeeds with me
to-night," he said. But his luck at play even
did not cure him of his restlessness; and he
started up after a while, pocketing his winnings,
and went off to a buffet, where he drank off
many bumpers of wine.

Here, as he was rattling away to the people
around him, laughing loudly and wild with spirits,
Dobbin found him. He had been to the card
tables to look there for his friend. Dobbin looked
as pale and grave as his comrade was flushed and
jovial.

"Hullo, Dob! Come and drink, old Dob! The
duke's wine is famous. Give me some more,
you sir;" and he held out a trembling glass for
the liquor.

"Come out, George," said Dobbin, still
gravely: "don't drink."

"Drink! there's nothing like it. Drink yourself, and light up your lantern jaws, old boy.
Here's to you."

Dobbin went up and whispered something to
him; at which George, giving a start and a wild
hurray, tossed off his glass, clapped it on the
table, and walked away speedily on his friend's
arm. "The enemy has passed the Sambre,"
William said, "and our left is already engaged.
Come away. We are to march in three hours."

Away went George, his nerves quivering with

excitement at the news so long looked for, so sudden when it came. What were love and intrigue now? He thought about a thousand things but these in his rapid walk to his quarters: his past life and future chances—the fate which might be before him—the wife, the child perhaps, from whom unseen he might be about to part. Oh, how he wished that night's work undone! and that with a clear conscience at least he might say farewell to the tender and guileless being by whose love he had set such little store.

He thought over his brief married life. In those few weeks he had frightfully dissipated his little capital. How wild and reckless he had been! Should any mischance befall him, what was then left for her? How unworthy he was of her! Why had he married her? He was not fit for marriage! Why had he disobeyed his father, who had been always so generous to him? Hope, remorse, ambition, tenderness, and selfish regret filled his heart. He sate down and wrote to his father, remembering what he had said once before, when he was engaged to fight a duel. Dawn faintly streaked the sky as he closed this farewell letter. He sealed it, and kissed the superscription. He thought how he had deserted that generous father, and of the thousand kindnesses which the stern old man had done him.

He had looked into Amelia's bedroom when he entered; she lay quiet, and her eyes seemed closed, and he was glad that she was asleep. On arriving at his quarters from the ball, he had found his regimental servant already making preparations for his departure: the man had understood his signal to be still, and these arrangements were very quickly and silently made. Should he go in and wake Amelia, he thought, or leave a note for her brother to break the news of departure to her? He went in to look at her once again.

She had been awake when he first entered her room, but had kept her eyes closed, so that even her wakefulness should not seem to reproach him. But when he had returned,—so soon after herself, too,—this timid little heart had felt more at ease; and turning towards him as he stept softly out of the room, she had fallen into a light sleep. George came in and looked at her again, entering still more softly. By the pale night-lamp he could see her sweet, pale face: the purple eyelids were fringed and closed, and one round arm, smooth and white, lay outside the coverlet. Good God! how pure she was; how gentle, how tender, and how friendless! and he, how selfish, brutal, and black with crime! Heart-stained and shamestricken, he stood at the bed's foot and looked at the sleeping girl. How dared he—who was he, to pray for one so spotless! God bless her! God bless her! He came to the bedside, and looked at the hand, the little soft hand, lying asleep; and he bent over the pillow noiselessly toward the gentle pale face.

Two fair arms closed tenderly around his neck as he stooped down. "I am awake, George," the poor child said, with a sob fit to break the little heart that nestled so closely by his own. She was awake, poor soul—and to what? At that moment a bugle from the Place of Arms began sounding clearly, and was taken up through the town; and 'midst the drums of the infantry, and the shrill pipes of the Scotch, the whole city awoke. . . .

All our friends took their share and fought like men in the great field. All day long, whilst the women were praying ten miles away, the lines of the dauntless English infantry were receiving and repelling the furious charges of the French horsemen. Guns which were heard at Brussels were plowing up their ranks, and comrades falling, and the resolute survivors closing in. Toward evening the attack of the French, repeated and resisted so bravely, slackened in its fury. They had other foes besides the British to engage, or were preparing for a final onset. It came at last: the columns of the Imperial Guard marched up the hill of Saint Jean, at length and at once to sweep the English from the height which they had maintained all day; and spite of all, unscared by the thunder of the artillery, which hurled death from the English line, the dark column prest on and up the hill. It seemed almost to crest the eminence, when it began to waver and falter. Then it stopt, still facing the shot. Then at last the English troops rushed from the post from which no enemy had been able to dislodge them, and the Guard turned and fled.

No more firing was heard at Brussels—the pursuit rolled miles away. Darkness came down on the field and city: and Amelia was praying for George, who was lying on his face, dead, with a bullet through his heart.

III

THE DEATH OF COLONEL NEWCOME [4]

CLIVE, and the boy sometimes with him, used to go daily to Grey Friars, where the colonel still lay ill. After some days the fever which had attacked him left him; but left him so weak and enfeebled that he could only go from his bed to the chair by his fireside. The season was exceedingly bitter; the chamber which he inhabited was warm and spacious: it was considered unadvisable to move him until he had attained greater strength and still warmer weather. The medical men of the House hoped he might rally in spring. My friend Dr. Goodenough came to him; he hoped too, but not with a hopeful face. A chamber, luckily vacant, hard by the colonel's, was assigned to his friends, where we sat when we were too many for him. Besides his customary attendants, he had two dear and watchful nurses, who were almost always with him—Ethel, and Madame de Florac, who had passed many a faithful year by an old man's bedside; who would have come, as to a work of religion, to any sick couch—much more to this one, where he lay for whose life she would once gladly have given her own.

But our colonel, we all were obliged to acknowledge, was no more our friend of old days. He knew us again, and was good to every one round him, as his wont was; especially when Boy came

[4] From "The Newcomes."

his old eyes lighted up with simple happiness, and with eager trembling hands he would seek under his bedclothes, or the pockets of his dressing-gown for toys or cakes, which he had caused to be purchased for his grandson. There was a little laughing, red-cheeked, white-headed gown-boy of the school, to whom the old man had taken a great fancy. One of the symptoms of his returning consciousness and recovery, as we hoped, was his calling for this child, who pleased our friend by his archness and merry ways; and who, to the old gentleman's unfailing delight, used to call him "Codd Colonel." "Tell little F—— that Codd Colonel wants to see him"; and the little gown-boy was brought to him: and the colonel would listen to him for hours, and hear all about his lessons and his play; and prattle, almost as childishly, about Dr. Raine and his own early school-days. The boys of the school, it must be said, had heard the noble old gentleman's touching history, and had all got to know and love him. They came every day to hear news of him; sent him in books and papers to amuse him; and some benevolent young souls—God's blessing on all honest boys, say I—painted theatrical characters and sent them in to Codd Colonel's grandson. The little fellow was made free of gown-boys, and once came thence to his grandfather in a little gown, which delighted the old man hugely. Boy said he would like to be a little gown-boy; and I make no doubt, when he is old enough, his father will get him that post, and put him under the tuition of my friend Dr. Senior.

So weeks passed away, during which our dear

old friend still remained with us. His mind was gone at intervals, but would rally feebly; and with his consciousness returned his love, his simplicity, his sweetness. He would talk French with Madame de Florac; at which time his memory appeared to awaken with surprizing vividness, his cheek flushed, and he was a youth again —a youth all love and hope—a stricken old man, with a beard as white as snow covering the noble careworn face. At such times he called her by her Christian name of Léonore; he addrest courtly old words of regard and kindness to the aged lady; anon he wandered in his talk, and spoke to her as if they were still young. Now, as in those early days, his heart was pure; no anger remained in it; no guile tainted it: only peace and good-will dwelt in it.

Rosey's death had seemed to shock him for a while when the unconscious little boy spoke of it. Before that circumstance, Clive had even forborne to wear mourning, lest the news should agitate his father. The colonel remained silent and was very much disturbed all that day, but he never appeared to comprehend the fact quite; and once or twice afterward asked why she did not come to see him? She was prevented, he supposed—she was prevented, he said, with a look of terror; he never once otherwise alluded to that unlucky tyrant of his household who had made his last years so unhappy.

The circumstance of Clive's legacy he never understood; but more than once spoke of Barnes to Ethel, and sent his compliments to him, and said he should like to shake him by the hand. Barnes Newcome never once offered to touch that honored hand, tho his sister bore her uncle's message to him. They came often from Bryanstone Square; Mrs. Hobson even offered to sit with the colonel, and read to him, and brought him books for his improvement. But her presence disturbed him; he cared not for her books: the two nurses whom he loved faithfully watched him; and my wife and I were admitted to him sometimes, both of whom he honored with regard and recognition. As for F. B., in order to be near his colonel, did not that good fellow take up his lodgings in Cistercian Lane, at the Red Cow? He is one whose errors, let us hope, shall be pardoned, *quia multum amavit.* I am sure he felt ten times more joy at hearing of Clive's legacy than if thousands had been bequeathed to himself. May good health and good fortune speed him!

The days went on; and our hopes, raised sometimes, began to flicker and fall. One evening the colonel left his chair for his bed in pretty good spirits; but passed a disturbed night, and the next morning was too weak to rise. Then he remained in his bed, and his friends visited him there. One afternoon he asked for his little gown-boy, and the child was brought to him, and sat by the bed with a very awe-stricken face; and then gathered courage, and tried to amuse him by telling him how it was a half-holiday, and they were having a cricket match with the St. Peter's boys in the green, and Grey Friars was in and winning. The colonel quite understood about it: he would like to see the game; he had played many a game on that green when he was a boy. He grew excited: Clive dismissed his father's little friend, and put a sovereign into his hand; and away he ran to say that Codd Colonel had come into a fortune, and to buy tarts, and to see the match out. *I, curre,* little white-haired gown-boy! Heaven speed you, little friend.

After the child had gone, Thomas Newcome began to wander more and more. He talked louder; he gave the word of command, spoke Hindustanee as if to his men. Then he spoke words in French rapidly, seizing a hand that was near him, and crying, "Toujours, toujours!" But it was Ethel's hand which he took. Ethel and Clive and the nurse were in the room with him; the nurse came to us, who were sitting in the adjoining apartment; Madame de Florac was there with my wife and Bayham.

At the look in the woman's countenance Madame de Florac started up. "He is very bad; he wanders a great deal," the nurse whispered. The French lady fell instantly on her knees, and remained rigid in prayer.

Some time afterward Ethel came in with a scared face to our pale group. "He is calling for you again, dear lady," she said, going up to Madame de Florac, who was still kneeling; "and just now he said he wanted Pendennis to take care of his boy. He will not know you." She hid her tears as she spoke.

She went into the room where Clive was at the bed's foot: the old man within it talked on rapidly for a while; then again he would sigh and be still; once more I heard him say hurriedly, "Take care of him when I'm in India"; and then with a heartrending voice he called out,

"Léonore, Léonore!" She was kneeling by his side now. The patient voice sank into faint murmurs; only a moan now and then announced that he was not asleep.

At the usual evening hour the chapel bell began to toll, and Thomas Newcome's hands outside the bed feebly beat time. And just as the last bell struck, a peculiar sweet smile shone over his face, and he lifted up his head a little, and quickly said, "Adsum!" and fell back. It was the word we used at school when names were called; and lo, he, whose heart was as that of a little child, had answered to his name, and stood in the presence of The Master.

IV

LONDON IN THE TIME OF THE FIRST GEORGE[5]

WE have brought our Georges to London city, and if we would behold its aspect may see it in Hogarth's lively perspective of Cheapside or read of it in a hundred contemporary books which paint the manners of that age. Our dear old Spectator looks smiling upon the streets, with their innumerable signs, and describes them with his charming humor. "Our streets are filled with Blue Boars, Black Swans, and Red Lions, not to mention Flying Pigs and Hogs in Armor, with other creatures more extraordinary than any in

[5] From the "Four Georges."

the deserts of Africa.'' A few of these quaint old figures still remain in London town. You may still see there, and over its old hostel in Ludgate Hill, the ''Belle Sauvage'' to whom the Spectator so pleasantly alludes in that paper; and who was, probably, no other than the sweet American Pocahontas,[6] who rescued from death the daring Captain Smith. There is the ''Lion's Head,'' down whose jaws the Spectator's own letters were passed; and over a great banker's in Fleet Street, the effigy of the wallet, which the founder of the firm bore when he came into London a country boy.

People this street, so ornamented, with crowds of swinging chairmen, with servants bawling to clear the way, with Mr. Dean in his cassock, his lackey marching before him; or Mrs. Dinah in her sack, tripping to chapel, her footboy carrying her ladyship's great prayer book; with itinerant tradesmen, singing their hundred cries (I remember forty years ago, as a boy in London city, a score of cheery, familiar cries that are silent now). Fancy the beaux thronging to the chocolate-houses, tapping their snuff-boxes as they issue thence, their periwigs appearing over the red curtains. Fancy Saccharissa,[7] beckoning and smiling from the upper windows, and a crowd of soldiers brawling and bustling at the door—

[6] Pocahontas, after her marriage with John Rolfe in 1616, went to England. She spent some time in London, but in March of the following year died at Gravesend. Her exact burial place is unknown.

[7] Saccharissa is the name under which Lady Dorothy Sidney is known through some of the poems of Waller, who wrote her praises under that name. She was of the family of Penshurst, to which belonged Sir Philip and Algernon Sidney.

gentlemen of the Life Guards, clad in scarlet, with blue facings, and laced with gold at the seams; gentlemen of the Horse Grenadiers, in their caps of sky-blue cloth, with the garter embroidered on the front in gold and silver; men of the Halberdiers, in their long red coats, as bluff Harry left them, with their ruff and velvet flat caps. Perhaps the King's Majesty himself is going to St. James's as we pass. If he is going to Parliament, he is in his coach-and-eight, surrounded by his guards and the high officers of his crown. Otherwise his Majesty only uses a chair, with six footmen walking before, and six yeomen of the guard at the sides of the sedan. The officers in waiting follow the king in coaches. It must be rather slow work.

Our *Spectator* and *Tatler* are full of delightful glimpses of the town life of those days. In the company of that charming guide, we may go to the opera, the comedy, the puppet show, the auction, even the cockpit; we can take boat at Temple Stairs, and accompany Sir Roger de Coverley and Mr. Spectator to Spring Garden— it will be called Vauxhall a few years hence, when Hogarth will paint for it. Would you not like to step back into the past, and be introduced to Mr. Addison?—not the Right Honorable Joseph Addison, Esq., George the First's Secretary of State, but to the delightful painter of contemporary manners; the man who, when in good humor himself, was the pleasantest companion in all England. I should like to go into Lockit's with him, and drink a bowl along with Sir R. Steele (who has just been knighted by King George, and who does not happen to have any money to pay his share of the reckoning). I should not care to follow Mr. Addison to his secretary's office in Whitehall. There we get into politics. Our business is pleasure, and the town, and the coffee-house, and the theater, and the Mall. Delightful Spectator! kind friend of leisure hours! happy companion! true Christian gentleman! How much greater, better, you are than the king Mr. Secretary kneels to!

You can have foreign testimony about old-world London, if you like; and my before-quoted friend, Charles Louis, Baron de Pöllnitz, will conduct us to it. "A man of sense," says he, "or a fine gentleman, is never at a loss for company in London, and this is the way the latter passes his time. He rises late, puts on a frock and, leaving his sword at home, takes his cane, and goes where he pleases. The park is commonly the place where he walks, because 'tis the Exchange for men of quality. 'Tis the same thing as the Tuileries at Paris, only the park has a certain beauty and simplicity which can not be described. The grand walk is called the Mall; is full of people at every hour of the day, but especially at morning and evening, when their Majesties often walk with the royal family, who are attended only by a half-dozen yeomen of the guard, and permit all persons to walk at the same time with them. The ladies and gentlemen always appear in rich dresses, for the English, who twenty years ago did not wear gold lace but in their army, are now embroidered and bedaubed as much as the French.

"I speak of persons of quality; for the citizen still contents himself with a suit of fine cloth, a good hat and wig, and fine linen. Everybody is well clothed here, and even the beggars don't make so ragged an appearance as they do elsewhere.'' After our friend, the man of quality, has had his morning or undress walk in the Mall, he goes home to dress, and then saunters to some coffee-house or chocolate-house frequented by the persons he would see. ''For 'tis a rule with the English to go once a day at least to houses of this sort, where they talk of business and news, read the papers, and often look at one another without opening their lips. And 'tis very well they are so mute; for were they all as talkative as people of other nations, the coffee-houses would be intolerable, and there would be no hearing what one man said where there are so many. The chocolate-house in St. James's Street, where I go every morning to pass away time, is always so full that a man can scarce turn about in it.''

Delightful as London city was, King George I liked to be out of it as much as ever he could; and when there, passed all his time with his Germans. It was with them as with Blucher, one hundred years afterward, when the bold old Reiter looked down from St. Paul's, and sighed out, *''Was für Plunder!''* The German women plundered; the German secretaries plundered; the German cooks and intendants plundered; even Mustapha and Mohammed, the German negroes, had a share of the booty. Take what you can get, was the old monarch's maxim. He was not a lofty monarch, certainly; he was not a patron of the fine arts; but he was not a hypocrite, he was not revengeful, he was not extravagant. Tho a despot in Hanover, he was a moderate ruler in England. His aim was to leave it to itself as much as possible, and to live out of it as much as he could. His heart was in Hanover. When taken ill on his last journey, as he was passing through Holland, he thrust his livid head out of the coach window, and gasped out "Osnaburg, Osnaburg!"

CHARLES DICKENS

Born in 1812, died in 1870; became a reporter in 1835; visited America in 1842 and again in 1867-68; published "Sketches by Boz" in 1836, "Pickwick Papers" in 1836-37, "Oliver Twist" in 1838, "Martin Chuzzelwit" in 1843, "David Copperfield" in 1849, "Tale of Two Cities" in 1859; many years after his death appeared his "Letters" in several volumes.

I

SIDNEY CARTON'S DEATH [1]

THEY said of him, about the city that night, that it was the peacefulest man's face ever beheld there. Many added that he looked sublime and prophetic.

One of the most remarkable sufferers by the same ax—a woman—had asked at the foot of the same scaffold, not long before, to be allowed to write down the thoughts that were inspiring her. If he had given any utterance to his, and they were prophetic, they would have been these:

"I see Barsad, and Cly, Defarge, the Vengeance, the Juryman, the Judge, long ranks of the new oppressors who have risen on the destruction of the old, perishing by his retributive instrument, before it shall cease out of its present use. I see a beautiful city and a brilliant people rising from this abyss, and, in their struggles to be

[1] The conclusion of "A Tale of Two Cities."

truly free, in their triumphs and defeats, through long, long years to come, I see the evil of this time and of the previous time of which this is the natural birth, gradually making expiation for itself and wearing out.

"I see the lives for which I lay down my life, peaceful, useful, prosperous and happy, in that England which I shall see no more. I see her with a child upon her bosom, who bears my name. I see her father, aged and bent, but otherwise restored, and faithful to all men in his healing office, and at peace. I see the good old man, so long their friend, in ten years' time enriching them with all he has, and passing tranquilly to his reward.

"I see that I hold a sanctuary in their hearts, and in the hearts of their descendants, generations hence. I see her, an old woman, weeping for me on the anniversary of this day. I see her and her husband, their course done, lying side by side in their last earthly bed, and I know that each was not more honored and held sacred in the other's soul than I was in the souls of both.

"I see that child who lay upon her bosom and who bore my name, a man winning his way up in that path of life which was once mine. I see him winning it so well, that my name is made illustrious there by the light of his. I see blots I threw upon it faded away. I see him, foremost of just judges and honored men, bringing a boy of my name, with a forehead that I know and golden hair, to this place—then fair to look upon, with not a trace of this day's disfigurement—and I hear him tell the child my story, with a tender and a faltering voice.

"It is a far, far better thing that I do than I have ever done; it is a far, far better rest that I go to than I have ever known."

II

BOB SAWYER'S PARTY [2]

WHEN the last "natural" had been declared, and the profit and loss account of fish and sixpences adjusted, to the satisfaction of all parties, Mr. Bob Sawyer rang for supper, and the visitors squeezed themselves into corners while it was getting ready.

It was not so easily got ready as some people may imagine. First of all, it was necessary to awaken the girl, who had fallen asleep with her face on the kitchen table; this took a little time, and, even when she did answer the bell, another quarter of an hour was consumed in fruitless endeavors to impart to her a faint and distant glimmering of reason. The man to whom the order for the oysters had been sent, had not been told to open them; it is a very difficult thing to open an oyster with a limp knife or a two-pronged fork, and very little was done in this way. Very little of the beef was done either; and the ham (which was also from the German sausage-shop round the corner) was in a similar predicament. However, there was plenty of porter in a tin can; and the cheese went a great

[2] From Chapter XXXI of "The Posthumous Papers of the Pickwick Club."

way, for it was very strong. So upon the whole, perhaps, the supper was quite as good as such matters usually are.

After supper another jug of punch was put upon the table, together with a paper of cigars, and a couple of bottles of spirits. Then there was an awful pause; and this awful pause was occasioned by a very common occurrence in this sort of places, but a very embarrassing one notwithstanding.

The fact is that the girl was washing the glasses. The establishment boasted four; we do not record the circumstance as at all derogatory to Mrs. Raddle, for there never was a lodging-house yet that was not short of glasses.

The landlady's glasses were little thin blown-glass tumblers, and those which had been borrowed from the public house were great, dropsical, bloated articles, each supported on a huge gouty leg. This would have been in itself sufficient to have possest the company with the real state of affairs; but the young woman of all work had prevented the possibility of any misconception arising in the mind of any gentlemen on the subject, by forcibly dragging every man's glass away, long before he had finished his beer, and audibly stating, despite the winks and interruptions of Mr. Bob Sawyer, that it was to be conveyed down-stairs, and washed forthwith.

It is a very ill wind that blows nobody any good. The prim man in the cloth boots, who had been unsuccessfully attempting to make a joke during the whole time the round game lasted, saw his opportunity, and availed himself of it. The instant the glasses disappeared he commenced a long story about a great public character, whose name he had forgotten, making a particular happy reply to another eminent and illustrious individual whom he had never been able to identify. He enlarged at some length and with great minuteness upon divers collateral circumstances, distantly connected with the anecdote in hand, but for the life of him he couldn't recollect at that precise moment what the anecdote was, altho he had been in the habit of telling the story with great applause for the last ten years.

"Dear me," said the prim man in the cloth boots, "it is a very extraordinary circumstance."

"I am sorry you have forgotten it," said Mr. Bob Sawyer, glancing eagerly at the door, as he thought he heard the noise of glasses jingling— "very sorry."

"So am I," responded the prim man, "because I know it would have afforded so much amusement. Never mind; I dare say I shall manage to recollect it, in the course of half an hour or so."

The prim man arrived at this point just as the glasses came back, when Mr. Bob Sawyer, who had been absorbed in attention during the whole time, said he should very much like to hear the end of it, for, so far as it went, it was, without exception, the very best story he had ever heard.

The sight of the tumblers restored Bob Sawyer to a degree of equanimity which he had not possest since his interview with his landlady. His face brightened up and he began to feel quite convivial.

"Now, Betsy," said Mr. Bob Sawyer, with

great suavity, and dispersing, at the same time, the tumultuous little mob of glasses that the girl had collected in the center of the table; "now, Betsy, the warm water: be brisk, there's a good girl."

"You can't have no warm water," replied Betsy.

"No warm water!" exclaimed Mr. Bob Sawyer.

"No," said the girl, with a shake of the head which exprest a more decided negative than the most copious language could have conveyed. "Missis Raddle said you warn't to have none."

The surprize depicted on the countenances of his guests imparted new courage to the host.

"Bring up the warm water instantly — instantly!" said Mr. Bob Sawyer, with desperate sternness.

"No; I can't," replied the girl; "Missis Raddle raked out the kitchen fire afore she went to bed, and locked up the kittle."

"Oh, never mind; never mind. Pray, don't disturb yourself about such a trifle," said Mr. Pickwick, observing the conflict of Bob Sawyer's passions, as depicted in his countenance, "cold water will do very well."

"Oh, admirably," said Mr. Benjamin Allen.

"My landlady is subject to some slight attacks of mental derangement," remarked Bob Sawyer with a ghastly smile; "I fear I must give her warning."

"No, don't," said Ben Allen.

"I fear I must," said Bob with heroic firmness. "I'll pay her what I owe her, and give her warning to-morrow morning." Poor fellow! how devoutly he wished he could!

Mr. Bob Sawyer's heart-sickening attempts to rally under this last blow communicated a dispiriting influence to the company, the greater part of whom, with the view of raising their spirits, attached themselves with extra cordiality to the cold brandy and water, the first perceptible effects of which were displayed in a renewal of hostilities between the scorbutic youth and the gentleman in the sanguine shirt. The belligerents vented their feelings of mutual contempt, for some time, in a variety of frownings and snortings, until at last the scorbutic youth felt it necessary to come to a more explicit understanding on the matter; when the following clear understanding took place.

"Sawyer," said the scorbutic youth.

"Well, Noddy," replied Mr. Bob Sawyer.

"I should be very sorry, Sawyer," said Mr. Noddy, "to create any unpleasantness at any friend's table, and much less at yours, Sawyer—very; but I must take this opportunity of informing Mr. Gunter that he is no gentleman."

"And I should be very sorry, Sawyer, to create any disturbance in the street in which you reside," said Mr. Gunter, "but I'm afraid I shall be under the necessity of alarming the neighbors by throwing the person who has just spoken, out o' window."

"What do you mean by that, Sir?" inquired Mr. Noddy.

"What I say, Sir," replied Mr. Gunter.

"I should like to see you do it, Sir," said Mr. Noddy.

"You shall feel me do it in half a minute, Sir," replied Mr. Gunter.

92

"I request that you'll favor me with your card, Sir," said Mr. Noddy.

"I'll do nothing of the kind, Sir," replied Mr. Gunter.

"Why not, Sir?" inquired Mr. Noddy.

"Because you'll stick it up over your chimney-piece, and delude your visitors into the false belief that a gentleman had been to see you, Sir," replied Mr. Gunter.

"Sir, a friend of mine shall wait on you in the morning," said Mr. Noddy.

"Sir, I'm very much obliged to you for the caution, and I'll leave particular directions with the servants to lock up the spoons," replied Mr. Gunter.

At this point the remainder of the guests interposed, and remonstrated with both parties on the impropriety of their conduct, on which Mr. Noddy begged to state that his father was quite as respectable as Mr. Gunter's father; to which Mr. Gunter replied that his father was to the full as respectable as Mr. Noddy's father, and that his father's son was as good a man as Mr. Noddy, any day in the week. As this announcement seemed the prelude to a recommencement of the dispute, there was another interference on the part of the company; and a vast quantity of talking and clamoring ensued, in the course of which Mr. Noddy gradually allowed his feelings to overpower him, and profest that he had ever entertained a devoted personal attachment toward Mr. Gunter. To this Mr. Gunter replied that, upon the whole, he rather preferred Mr. Noddy to his own brother; on hearing which admission, Mr. Noddy magnanimously rose from his seat, and proferred his hand to Mr. Gunter. Mr. Gunter grasped it with affecting fervor; and everybody said that the whole dispute had been conducted in a manner which was highly honorable to both parties concerned.

"Now," said Jack Hopkins, "just to set us going again, Bob, I don't mind singing a song." And Hopkins, incited thereto by tumultuous applause, plunged himself at once into "The King, God Bless Him," which he sang as loud as he could, to a novel air, compounded to the "Bay of Biscay," and "A Frog He Would." The chorus was the essence of the song, and, as each gentleman sang it to the tune he knew best, the effect was very striking indeed.

It was at the end of the chorus to the first verse, that Mr. Pickwick held up his hand in a listening attitude, and said, as soon as silence was restored:

"Hush! I beg your pardon. I thought I heard somebody calling from up-stairs."

A profound silence immediately ensued; and Mr. Bob Sawyer was observed to turn pale.

"I think I hear it now," said Mr. Pickwick. "Have the goodness to open the door."

The door was no sooner opened than all doubt on the subject was removed.

"Mr. Sawyer—Mr. Sawyer," screamed a voice from the two-pair landing.

"It's my landlady," said Bob Sawyer, looking around him with great dismay. "Yes, Mrs. Raddle."

"What do you mean by this, Mr. Sawyer?" replied the voice, with great shrillness and rapidity of utterance. "Ain't it enough to be swindled out of one's rent, and money lent out of pocket besides, and abused and insulted by your friends that dares to call themselves men, without having the house turned out of window, and noise enough made to bring the fire-engines here, at two o'clock in the morning? Turn them wretches away.''

"You ought to be ashamed of yourselves,'' said the voice of Mr. Raddle, which appeared to proceed from beneath some distant bed-clothes.

"Ashamed of themselves!'' said Mrs. Raddle. "Why don't you go down and knock 'em every one down-stairs? You would if you was a man.''

"I should if I was a dozen men, my dear,'' replied Mr. Raddle, pacifically, "but they've rather the advantage of me in numbers, my dear.''

"Ugh, you coward!'' replied Mrs. Raddle, with supreme contempt. "Do you mean to turn them wretches out, or not, Mr. Sawyer?''

"They're going, Mrs. Raddle, they're going,'' said the miserable Bob. "I am afraid you'd better go,'' said Mr. Bob Sawyer to his friends. "I thought you were making too much noise.''

"It's a very unfortunate thing,'' said the prim man. "Just as we were getting so comfortable too!'' The fact was the prim man was just beginning to have a dawning recollection of the story he had forgotten.

"It's hardly to be borne,'' said the prim man, looking round. "Hardly to be borne, is it?''

"Not to be endured,'' replied Jack Hopkins; "let's have the other verse, Bob. Come, here goes.''

"No, no, Jack, don't,'' interposed Bob Sawyer;

"it's a capital song, but I am afraid we had better not have the other verse. They are very violent people, the people of the house."

"Shall I step up-stairs, and pitch into the landlord?" inquired Hopkins, "or keep on ringing the bell, or go and groan on the staircase? You may command me, Bob."

"I am very much indebted to you for your friendship and good nature, Hopkins," said the wretched Mr. Bob Sawyer, "but I think the best plan to avoid any further dispute is for us to break up at once."

"Now, Mr. Sawyer," screamed the shrill voice of Mrs. Raddle, "are them brutes going?"

"They're only looking for their hats, Mrs. Raddle," said Bob; "they are going directly."

"Going!" said Mrs. Raddle, thrusting her nightcap over the banisters just as Mr. Pickwick, followed by Mr. Tupman, emerged from the sitting-room. "Going! What did they ever come for?"

"My dear ma'am," remonstrated Mr. Pickwick, looking up.

"Get along with you, you old wretch!" replied Mrs. Raddle, hastily withdrawing the nightcap. "Old enough to be his grandfather, you villain! You're worse than any of 'em."

Mr. Pickwick found it in vain to protest his innocence, so hurried down-stairs into the street, whither he was closely followed by Mr. Tupman, Mr. Winkle, and Mr. Snodgrass. Mr. Ben Allen, who was dismally deprest with spirits and agitation, accompanied them as far as London Bridge, and in the course of the walk confided to Mr. Winkle, as an especially sensible person to entrust the secret to, that he was resolved to cut the throat of any gentleman except Mr. Bob Sawyer who should aspire to the affections of his sister Arabella. Having exprest his determination to perform this painful duty of a brother with proper firmness, he burst into tears, knocked his hat over his eyes, and making the best of his way back, knocked double knocks at the door of the Borough Market, and took short naps on the steps alternately, until daybreak, under the firm impression that he lived there, and had forgotten the key.

The visitors having all departed, in compliance with the rather pressing request of Mrs. Raddle, the luckless Mr. Bob Sawyer was left alone to meditate on the probable events of the morrow, and the pleasures of the evening.

III

DICK SWIVELLER AND THE MAR-CHIONESS [3]

As these games were very silently conducted, notwithstanding the magnitude of the interests involved, Mr. Swiveller began to think that on those evenings when Mr. and Miss Brass were out (and they often went out now) he heard a kind of snorting or hard-breathing sound in the direction of the door, which it occurred to him, after some reflection, must proceed from the small

[3] From Chapters LVII and LVIII of "The Old Curiosity Shop."

servant, who always had a cold from damp living. Looking intently that way one night, he plainly distinguished an eye gleaming and glistening at the keyhole; and having now no doubt that his suspicions were correct, he stole softly to the door, and pounced upon her before she was aware of his approach.

"Oh! I didn't mean any harm indeed. Upon my word I didn't," cried the small servant, struggling like a much larger one. "It's so very dull, down-stairs. Please don't you tell upon me; please don't."

"Tell upon you!" said Dick. "Do you mean to say you were looking through the keyhole for company?"

"Yes, upon my word I was," replied the small servant.

"How long have you been cooling your eye there?" said Dick.

"Oh, ever since you first began to play them cards, and long before."

Vague recollections of several fantastic exercises with which he had refreshed himself after the fatigues of business, and to all of which, no doubt, the small servant was a party, rather disconcerted Mr. Swiveller; but he was not very sensitive on such points, and recovered himself speedily.

"Well—come in," he said, after a little consideration. "Here—sit down, and I'll teach you how to play."

"Oh! I durstn't do it," rejoined the small servant; "Miss Sally 'ud kill me, if she know'd I came up here."

"Have you got a fire down-stairs?" said Dick.

"A very little one," replied the small servant.

"Miss Sally couldn't kill me if she know'd I went down there, so I'll come," said Richard, putting the cards into his pocket. "Why, how thin you are! What do you mean by it?"

"It ain't my fault."

"Could you eat any bread and meat?" said Dick, taking down his hat. "Yes? Ah! I thought so. Did you ever taste beer?"

"I had a sip of it once," said the small servant.

"Here's a state of things!" cried Mr. Swiveller, raising his eyes to the ceiling. "She never tasted it—it can't be tasted in a sip! Why, how old are you?"

"I don't know."

Mr. Swiveller opened his eyes very wide, and appeared thoughtful for a moment; then, bidding the child mind the door until he came back, vanished straightway.

Presently he returned, followed by the boy from the public house, who bore in one hand a plate of bread and beef, and in the other a great pot, filled with some very fragrant compound, which sent forth a grateful steam, and was indeed choice purl, made after a particular recipe which Mr. Swiveller had imparted to the landlord at a period when he was deep in his books and desirous to conciliate his friendship. Relieving the boy of his burden at the door, and charging his little companion to fasten it to prevent surprize, Mr. Swiveller followed her into the kitchen.

"There!" said Richard, putting the plate before her. "First of all, clear that off, and then you'll see what's next."

The small servant needed no second bidding, and the plate was soon empty.

"Next," said Dick, handing the purl, "take a pull at that; but moderate your transports, for you're not used to it. Well, is it good?"

"Oh! isn't it?" said the small servant.

Mr. Swiveller appeared gratified beyond all expression by this reply, and took a long draft himself, stedfastly regarding his companion while he did so. These preliminaries disposed of, he applied himself to teaching her the game, which she soon learned tolerably well, being both sharp-witted and cunning.

"Now," said Mr. Swiveller, putting two six-pences into a saucer and trimming the wretched candle, when the cards had been cut and dealt, "those are the stakes. If you win you get 'em all. If I win, I get 'em. To make it seem more real and pleasant, I shall call you the Marchioness, do you hear?"

The small servant nodded.

"Then, Marchioness," said Mr. Swiveller, "fire away!"

The Marchioness, holding her cards very tight in both hands, considered which to play, and Mr. Swiveller, assuming the gay and fashionable air which such society required, took another pull at the tankard, and waited for her lead."

Mr. Swiveller and his partner played several rubbers with varying success, until the loss of three sixpences, the gradual sinking of the purl, and the striking of ten o'clock, combined to render that gentleman mindful of the flight of time, and the expediency of withdrawing before Mr. Sampson and Miss Sally Brass returned.

"With which object in view, Marchioness," said Mr. Swiveller gravely, "I shall ask your ladyship's permission to put the board in my pocket, and to retire from the presence when I have finished this tankard; merely observing, Marchioness, that since life like a river is flowing, I care not how fast it rolls on, ma'am, on, while such purl on the bank still is growing, and such eyes light the waves as they run. Marchioness, your health. You will excuse my wearing my hat, but the palace is damp, and the marble floor is—if I may be allowed the expression—sloppy."

As a precaution against this latter inconvenience, Mr. Swiveller had been sitting for some time with his feet on the hob, in which attitude he now gave utterance of these apologetic observations, and slowly sipped the last choice drops of nectar.

"The Baron Sampsono Brasso and his fair sister are (you tell me) at the play?" said Mr. Swiveller, leaning his left arm heavily upon the table, and raising his voice and his right leg after the manner of a theatrical bandit.

The Marchioness nodded.

"Ha!" said Mr. Swiveller, with a portentous frown. "'Tis well. Marchioness!—but no matter. Some wine there. Ho!" He illustrated these melodramatic morsels by handing the tankard to himself with great humility, receiving it haughtily, drinking from it thirstily, and smacking his lips fiercely.

The small servant, who was not so well acquainted with theatrical conventionalities as Mr. Swiveller (having indeed never seen a play, or heard one spoken of, except by chance through chinks of doors and in other forbidden places), was rather alarmed by demonstrations so novel in their nature, and showed her concern so plainly in her looks that Mr. Swiveller felt it necessary to discharge his brigand manner for one more suitable to private life, as he asked:

"Do they often go where glory waits 'em, and leave you here?"

"Oh, yes; I believe you they do," returned the small servant. "Miss Sally's such a one-er for that, she is."

"Such a what?" said Dick.

"Such a one-er," returned the Marchioness.

After a moment's reflection, Mr. Swiveller determined to forego his responsible duty of setting her right, and to suffer her to talk on; as it was evident that her tongue was loosened by the purl, and her opportunities for conversation were not so frequent as to render a momentary check of little consequence.

"They sometimes go to see Mr. Quilp," said the small servant with a shrewd look, "they go to a many places, bless you."

"Is Mr. Brass a wunner?" said Dick.

"Not half what Miss Sally is, he isn't," replied the small servant, shaking her head. "Bless you, he'd never do anything without her."

"Oh! He wouldn't, wouldn't he?" said Dick.

"Miss Sally keeps him in such order," said the small servant; "he always asks her advice, he does; and he catches it sometimes. Bless you, you wouldn't believe how much he catches it."

"I suppose," said Dick, "that they consult together a good deal, and about a great many people—about me, for instance, sometimes, eh?"

The Marchioness nodded amazingly.

"Complimentary?" said Mr. Swiveller.

The Marchioness changed the motion of her head, which had not yet left off nodding, and suddenly began to shake it from side to side with vehemence which threatened to dislocate her neck.

"Humph!" Dick muttered. "Would it be any breach of confidence, Marchioness, to relate what they say of the humble individual who has now the honor to—?"

"Miss Sally says you're a funny chap," replied his friend.

"Well, Marchioness," said Mr. Swiveller, "that's not uncomplimentary. Merriment, Marchioness, is not a bad or degrading quality. Old King Cole was him a merry old soul, if we may put any faith in the pages of history."

"But she says," pursued his companion, "that you an't to be trusted."

"Why, really, Marchioness," said Mr. Swiveller, thoughtfully, "several ladies and gentlemen—not exactly professional persons, but tradespeople, ma'am, tradespeople—have made the same remark. The obscure citizen who keeps the hotel over the way, inclined strongly to that opinion to-night when I ordered him to prepare the banquet. It's a popular prejudice, Marchioness; and yet I am sure I don't know why, for I have been trusted in my time to a considerable amount, and I can safely say that I never forsook my trust until it deserted me—never. Mr. Brass is of the same opinion, I suppose?"

His friend nodded again, with a cunning look which seemed to hint that Mr. Brass held stronger opinions on the subject than his sister; and seeming to recollect herself, added imploringly, "But don't you ever tell upon me, or I shall be beat to death."

"Marchioness," said Mr. Swiveller, rising, "the word of a gentleman is as good as his bond —sometimes better; as in the present case, where his bond might prove but a doubtful sort of security. I am your friend, and I hope we shall play many more rubbers together in this same saloon. But, Marchioness," added Richard, stopping in his way to the door, and wheeling slowly round upon the small servant, who was following with the candle; "it occurs to me that you must be in the constant habit of airing your eye at keyholes, to know all this."

"I only wanted," replied the trembling Marchioness, "to know where the key of the safe was hid; that was all; and I wouldn't have taken much if I had found it—only enough to squench my hunger."

"You didn't find it then?" said Dick. "But of course you didn't, or you'd be plumper. Good night, Marchioness. Fare thee well, and if forever, then forever fare thee well—and put up the chain, Marchioness, in case of accidents."

IV

A HAPPY RETURN OF THE DAY [4]

MR. and Mrs. Wilfer had seen a full quarter of a hundred more anniversaries of their wedding-day than Mr. and Mrs. Lammle had seen of theirs, but they still celebrated the occasion in the bosom of their family. Not that these celebrations ever resulted in anything particularly agreeable, or that the family was ever disappointed by that circumstance on account of having looked forward to the return of the auspicious day with sanguine anticipations of enjoyment. It was kept morally, rather as a Fast than a Feast, enabling Mrs. Wilfer to hold a somber darkling state, which exhibited that impressive woman in her choicest colors.

The noble lady's condition on these delightful occasions was one compounded of heroic endurance and heroic forgiveness. Lurid indications of the better marriages she might have made, shone athwart the awful gloom of her composure, and fitfully revealed the cherub as a little monster unaccountably favored by Heaven, who had possest himself of a blessing, for which many of his superiors had sued and contended in vain. So firmly had this his position toward his treasure become established, that when the anniversary arrived, it always found him in an apologetic state. It is not impossible that his modest penitence may have even gone the length of sometimes

[4] From Book III, Chapter IV, of "Our Mutual Friend."

severely reproving him for that he ever took the liberty of making so exalted a character his wife.

As for the children of the union, their experience of these festivals had been sufficiently uncomfortable to lead them annually to wish, when out of their tenderest years, either that Ma had married somebody else instead of much-teased Pa, or that Pa had married somebody else instead of Ma.

When there came to be but two sisters left at home, the daring mind of Bella on the next of these occasions scaled the height of wondering with droll vexation, "what on earth Pa ever could have seen in Ma, to induce him to make such a little fool of himself as to ask her to have him."

The revolving year now bringing the day round in its orderly sequence, Bella arrived in the Boffin chariot to assist at the celebration. It was the family custom when the day recurred to sacrifice a pair of fowls on the altar of Hymen; and Bella had sent a note beforehand, to intimate that she would bring the votive offering with her. So, Bella and the fowls, by the united energies of two horses, two men, four wheels, and a plum-pudding carriage dog with as uncomfortable a collar on as if he had been George the Fourth, were deposited at the door of the parental dwelling. They were there received by Mrs. Wilfer in person, whose dignity on this, as on most special occasions, was heightened by a mysterious toothache.

"I shall not require the carriage at night," said Bella. "I shall walk back."

The male domestic of Mrs. Boffin touched his hat, and in the act of departure had an awful glare bestowed upon him by Mrs. Wilfer, intended to carry deep into his audacious soul the assurance that, whatever his private suspicions might be, male domestics in livery were no rarity there.

"Well, dear Ma," said Bella, "and how do you do?"

"I am as well, Bella," replied Mrs. Wilfer, "as can be expected."

"Dear me, Ma," said Bella, "you talk as if one was just born!"

"That's exactly what Ma has been doing," interposed Lavvy, over the maternal shoulder, "ever since we got up this morning. It's all very well to laugh, Bella, but anything more exasperating it is impossible to conceive."

Mrs. Wilfer, with a look too full of majesty to be accompanied by any words, attended both her daughters to the kitchen, where the sacrifice was to be prepared.

"Mr. Rokesmith," said she, resignedly, "has been so polite as to place his sitting-room at our disposal to-day. You will therefore, Bella, be entertained in the humble abode of your parents, so far in accordance with your present style of living, that there will be a drawing-room for your reception as well as a dining-room. Your papa invited Mr. Rokesmith to partake of our lowly fare. In excusing himself on account of a particular engagement, he offered the use of his apartment."

Bella happened to know that he had no engagement out of his own room at Mr. Boffin's, but she approved of his staying away. "We should only have put one another out of countenance," she thought, "and we do that quite often enough as it is."

Yet she had sufficient curiosity about his room to run up to it with the least possible delay, and make a close inspection of its contents. It was tastefully tho economically furnished, and very neatly arranged. There were shelves and stands of books, English, French, and Italian; and in a portfolio on the writing-table there were sheets upon sheets of memoranda and calculations in figures, evidently referring to the Boffin property. On that table also, carefully backed with canvas, varnished, mounted, and rolled like a map, was the placard descriptive of the murdered man who had come from afar to be her husband. She shrank from this ghostly surprize, and felt quite frightened as she rolled and tied it up again. Peeping about here and there, she came upon a print, a graceful head of a pretty woman, elegantly framed, hanging in the corner by the easy chair. "Oh, indeed, Sir!" said Bella, after stopping to ruminate before it. "Oh, indeed, Sir! I fancy I can guess whom you think that's like. But I'll tell you what it's much more like—your impudence!" Having said which she decamped: not solely because she was offended, but because there was nothing else to look at.

"Now, Ma," said Bella, reappearing in the kitchen with some remains of a blush, "you and Lavvy think magnificent me fit for nothing, but I intend to prove the contrary. I mean to be cook to-day."

"Hold!" rejoined her majestic mother. "I can not permit it. Cook in that dress!"

"As for my dress, Ma," returned Bella, merrily searching in a dresser-drawer, "I mean to apron it and towel it all over the front; and as to permission, I mean to do without."

"You cook?" said Mrs. Wilfer. "You who never cooked when you were at home?"

"Yes, Ma," returned Bella; "that is precisely the state of the case."

She girded herself with a white apron, and busily with knots and pins contrived a bib to it, coming close and tight under her chin, as if it had caught her round the neck to kiss her. Over this bib her dimples looked delightful, and under it her pretty figure not less so. "Now, Ma," said Bella, pushing back her hair from her temples with both hands, "what's first?"

"First," returned Mrs. Wilfer solemnly, "if you persist in what I can not but regard as conduct utterly incompatible with the equipage in which you arrived—"

("Which I do, Ma.")

"First, then, you put the fowls down to the fire."

"To—be—sure!" cried Bella; "and flour them, and twirl them around, and there they go!" sending them spinning at a great rate. "What's next, Ma?"

"Next," said Mrs. Wilfer with a wave of her gloves, expressive of abdication under protest from the culinary throne, "I would recommend examination of the bacon in the saucepan on the fire, and also of the potatoes by the application of a fork. Preparation of the greens will further become necessary if you persist in this unseemly demeanor."

"As of course I do, Ma."

Persisting, Bella gave her attention to one thing and forgot the other, and gave her attention to the other and forgot the third, and remembering the third was distracted by the fourth, and made amends whenever she went wrong by giving the unfortunate fowls an extra spin, which made their chance of ever getting cooked exceedingly doubtful. But it was pleasant cookery too. Meanwhile Miss Lavinia, oscillating between the kitchen and the opposite room, prepared the dining-table in the latter chamber. This office she (always doing her household spiriting with unwillingness) performed in a startling series of whisks and bumps; laying the table-cloth as if she were raising the wind, putting down the glasses and salt-cellars as if she were knocking at the door, and clashing the knives and forks in a skirmishing manner suggestive of hand-to-hand conflict.

"Look at Ma," whispered Lavinia to Bella when this was done, and they stood over the roasting fowls. "If one was the most dutiful child in existence (of course, on the whole, one hopes one is), isn't she enough to make one want to poke her with something wooden, sitting there bolt upright in the corner?"

"Only suppose," returned Bella, "that poor Pa was to sit bolt upright in another corner."

"My dear, he couldn't do it," said Lavvy. "Pa would loll directly. But indeed I do not believe there ever was any human creature who could keep so bolt upright as Ma, or put such an amount of aggravation into one back! What's the matter, Ma? Ain't you well, Ma?"

"Doubtless I am very well," returned Mrs.

Wilfer, turning her eyes upon her youngest born, with scornful fortitude. "What should be the matter with me?"

"You don't seem very brisk, Ma," retorted Lavvy the bold.

"Brisk?" repeated her parent. "Brisk? Whence the low expression, Lavinia? If I am uncomplaining, if I am silently contented with my lot, let that suffice for my family."

"Well, Ma," returned Lavvy, "since you will force it out of me, I must respectfully take leave to say that your family are no doubt under the greatest obligations to you for having an annual toothache on your wedding-day, and that it's very disinterested in you, and an immense blessing to them. Still, on the whole, it is impossible to be too boastful even of that boon."

"You incarnation of sauciness," said Mrs. Wilfer, "do you speak like that to me? On this day of all days in the year? Pray do you know what would have become of you, if I had not bestowed my hand upon R. W., your father, on this day?"

"No, Ma," replied Lavvy, "I really do not; and, with the greatest respect for your abilities and information, I very much doubt if you do either."

Whether or no the sharp vigor of this sally on a weak point of Mrs. Wilfer's entrenchments might have routed that heroine for the time, is rendered uncertain by the arrival of a flag of truce in the person of Mr. George Sampson: bidden to the feast as a friend of the family, whose affections were now understood to be in course of transference from Bella to Lavinia, and whom Lavinia kept—possibly in remembrance of his bad taste in having overlooked her in the first instance—under a course of stinging discipline.

"I congratulate you, Mrs. Wilfer," said Mr. George Sampson, who had meditated this neat address while coming along, "on the day." Mrs. Wilfer thanked him with a magnanimous sigh, and again became an unresisting prey to that inscrutable toothache.

"I am surprized," said Mr. Sampson feebly, "that Miss Bella condescends to cook."

Here Miss Lavinia descended on the ill-starred young gentleman with a crushing supposition that at all events it was no business of his. This disposed of Mr. Sampson in a melancholy retirement of spirit, until the cherub arrived, whose amazement at the lovely woman's occupation was great.

However, she persisted in dishing the dinner as well as cooking it, and then sat down, bibless and apronless, to partake of it as an illustrious guest: Mrs. Wilfer first responding to her husband's cheerful "For what we are about to receive—" with a sepulchral Amen, calculated to cast a damp upon the stoutest appetite.

"But what," said Bella, as she watched the carving of the fowls, "makes them pink inside, I wonder, Pa! Is it the breed?"

"No; I don't think it's the breed, my dear," returned Pa. "I rather think it is because they are not done."

"They ought to be," said Bella.

"Yes, I'm aware they ought to be, my dear," rejoined her father, "but they—ain't."

So, the gridiron was put in requisition, and the good-tempered cherub, who was often as un-cherubically employed in his own family as if he had been in the employment of some of the Old Masters, undertook to grill the fowls. Indeed, except in respect of staring about him (a branch of the public service to which the pictorial cherub is much addicted), this domestic cherub discharged as many odd functions as his prototype; with the difference, say, that he performed with a blacking-brush on the family's boots, instead of performing on enormous wind instruments and double-basses, and that he conducted himself with cheerful alacrity to much useful purpose, instead of foreshortening himself in the air with the vaguest intentions.

Bella helped him with his supplemental cookery, and made him very happy, but put him in mortal terror too by asking him when they sat down at table again, how he supposed they cooked fowls at the Greenwich dinner, and whether he believed they really were such pleasant dinners as people said? His secret winks and nods of remonstrance, in reply, made the mischievous Bella laugh until she choked, and then Lavinia was obliged to slap her on the back, and then she laughed the more.

But her mother was a fine corrective at the other end of the table; to whom her father, in the innocence of his good fellowship, at intervals appealed with: "My dear, I am afraid you are not enjoying yourself?"

"Why so, R. W.?" she would sonorously reply.

"Because, my dear, you seem a little out of sorts."

"Not at all," would be the rejoinder, in exactly the same tone.

"Would you take a merry-thought, my dear?"

"Thank you. I will take whatever you please, R. W."

"Well, but my dear, do you like it?"

"I like it as well as I like anything, R. W." The stately woman would then, with a meritorious appearance of devoting herself to the general good, pursue her dinner as if she were feeding somebody else on high public grounds.

Bella had brought dessert and two bottles of wine, thus shedding unprecedented splendor on the occasion. Mrs. Wilfer did the honors of the first glass by proclaiming: "R. W., I drink to you."

"Thank you, my dear. And I to you."

"Pa and Ma!" said Bella.

"Permit me," Mrs. Wilfer interposed, with outstretched glove. "No. I think not. I drank to your Pa. If, however, you insist on including me, I can in gratitude offer no objection."

"Why, Lor, Ma," interposed Lavvy the bold, "isn't it the day that made you and Pa one and the same? I have no patience."

"By whatever other circumstances the day may be marked, it is not the day, Lavinia, on which I will allow a child of mine to pounce upon me. I beg—nay, command!—that you will not pounce. R. W., it is appropriate to recall that it is for you to command and for me to obey."

"It is your house, and you are master at your own table. Both our healths!" Drinking the toast with tremendous stiffness.

"I really am a little afraid, my dear," hinted

the cherub meekly, "that you are not enjoying
yourself?"

"On the contrary," returned Mrs. Wilfer,
"quite so. Why should I not?"

"I thought, my dear, that perhaps your face
might—"

"My face might be a martyrdom, but what
would that import, or who should know it if I
smiled?"

And she did smile; manifestly freezing the
blood of Mr. George Sampson by so doing. For
that young gentleman, catching her smiling eye,
was so very much appalled by its expression as to
cast in his thoughts concerning what he had done
to bring it down upon himself.

"The mind naturally falls," said Mrs. Wilfer,
"shall I say into a reverie, or shall I say into a
retrospect? on a day like this."

Lavvy, sitting with defiantly folded arms, replied (but not audibly), "For goodness' sake
say whichever of the two you like best, Ma, and
get it over."

"The mind," pursued Mrs. Wilfer in an
oratorical manner, "naturally reverts to Papa
and Mama—I here allude to my parents—at
a period before the earliest dawn of this day.
I was considered tall; perhaps I was. Papa
and Mama were unquestionably tall. I have
rarely seen a finer woman than my mother;
never than my father."

The irrepressible Lavvy remarked aloud,
"Whatever grandpapa was, he wasn't a female."

"Your grandpapa," retorted Mrs. Wilfer, with
an awful look, and in an awful tone, "was what
I describe him to have been, and would have

struck any of his grandchildren to the earth who presumed to question it. It was one of Mama's cherished hopes that I should become united to a tall member of society. It may have been a weakness, but if so, it was equally the weakness, I believe, of King Frederick of Prussia." These remarks being offered to Mr. George Sampson, who had not the courage to come out for single combat, but lurked with his chest under the table and his eyes cast down, Mrs. Wilfer proceeded, in a voice of increasing sternness and impressiveness, until she should force that skulker to give himself up. "Mama would appear to have had an indefinable foreboding of what afterward happened, for she would frequently urge upon me, 'Not a little man. Promise me, my child, not a little man. Never, never, never marry a little man!' Papa also would remark to me (he possest extraordinary humor), 'That a family of whales must not ally themselves with sprats.'

"His company was eagerly sought, as may be supposed, by the wits of the day, and our house was their continual resort. I have known as many as three copper-plate engravers exchanging the most exquisite sallies and retorts there, at one time." (Here Mr. Sampson delivered himself captive, and said, with an uneasy movement on his chair, that three was a large number, and it must have been highly entertaining). "Among the most prominent members of that distinguished circle, was a gentleman measuring six feet four in height. He was not an engraver." (Here Mr. Sampson said, with no reason whatever, of course not.) "This gentleman was so obliging as to honor me with attentions which I could not fail to understand.'' (Here Mr. Sampson murmured that when it came to that, you could always tell.) ''I immediately announced to both parents that those attentions were misplaced, and that I could not favor his suit. They inquired was he too tall? I replied it was not the stature, but the intellect was too lofty. At our house, I said, the tone was too brilliant, the pressure was too high, to be maintained by me, a mere woman, in every-day domestic life. I well remember Mama's clasping her hands, and exclaiming, 'This will end in a little man!' '' (Here Mr. Sampson glanced at his host and shook his head with despondency.) ''She afterward went so far as to predict that it would end in a little man whose mind would be below the average, but that was in what I may denominate a paroxysm of maternal disappointment. Within a month,'' said Mrs. Wilfer, deepening her voice, as if she were relating a terrible ghost story, ''within a month, I first saw R. W., my husband. Within a year I married him. It is natural for the mind to recall these dark coincidences on the present day.''

Mr. Sampson, at length released from the custody of Mrs. Wilfer's eye, now drew a long breath, and made the original and striking remark, that there was no accounting for these sort of presentiments. R. W. scratched his head and looked apologetically all round the table until he came to his wife, when observing her as it were shrouded in a more somber veil than before, he once more hinted, ''My dear, I am really afraid you are not altogether enjoying yourself?" To which she once more replied, "On the contrary, R. W. Quite so."

The wretched Mr. Sampson's position at this agreeable entertainment was truly pitiable. For, not only was he exposed defenseless to the harangues of Mrs. Wilfer, but he received the utmost contumely at the hands of Lavinia, who, partly to show Bella that she (Lavinia) could do what she liked with him, and partly to pay him off for still obviously admiring Bella's beauty, led him the life of a dog. Illuminated on the one hand by the stately graces of Mrs. Wilfer's oratory, and shadowed on the other by the cheeks and frowns of the young lady to whom he had devoted himself in his destitution, the sufferings of this young gentleman were distressing to witness. If his mind for the moment reeled under them, it may be urged, in extenuation of its weakness, that it was constitutionally a knock-knee'd mind, and never very strong upon its legs.

CHARLOTTE BRONTE

Born in 1816, died in 1855; her father a curate with whom
most of her life was spent; married Rev. A. Nicholls, who
survived her fifty years; published "Jane Eyre" in 1847,
"Shirley" in 1849, "The Professor" in 1855, and "Poems"
in 1846.

OF THE AUTHOR OF "VANITY FAIR"[1]

To that class in whose eyes whatever is unusual is wrong; whose ears detect in each protest
against bigotry—that parent of crime—an insult
to piety, that regent of God on earth, I would
suggest to such doubters certain obvious distinc-
tions; I would remind them of certain simple
truths.

Conventionality is not morality. Self-
righteousness is not religion. To attack the first
is not to assail the last. To pluck the mask from
the face of the Pharisee is not to lift an impious
hand to the crown of thorns. These things
and deeds are diametrically opposed; they are
as distinct as vice from virtue. Men too often
confound them: they should not be confounded:
appearance should not be mistaken for truth;
narrow human doctrines, that only tend to elate

[1] Preface to the second edition of "Jane Eyre." "Vanity
Fair" and "Jane Eyre" were published contemporaneously—
"Vanity Fair" (serially) in 1846-48, and "Jane Eyre" in
1847.

and magnify a few, should not be substituted for the world-redeeming creed of Christ. There is—I repeat it—a difference; and it is a good, and not a bad action to mark broadly and clearly the line of separation between them.

The world may not like to see these ideas dissevered, for it has been accustomed to blend them; finding it convenient to make external show pass for sterling worth—to let white-washed walls vouch for clean shrines. It may hate him who dares to scrutinize and expose —to raze the gilding, and show base metal under it—to penetrate the sepulcher, and reveal charnel relics: but hate as it will, it is indebted to him.

Ahab did not like Micaiah, because he never prophesied good concerning him, but evil: probably he liked the sycophant son of Chenaanah better; yet might Ahab have escaped a bloody death, had he but stopt his ears to flattery, and opened them to faithful counsel.

There is a man in our own days whose words are not framed to tickle delicate ears; who, to my thinking, comes before the great ones of society much as the son of Imlah came before the throned kings of Judah and Israel; and who speaks truth as deep, with a power as prophet-like and as vital—a mien as dauntless and as daring. Is the satirist of "Vanity Fair" admired in high places? I can not tell; but I think if some of those amongst whom he hurls the Greek-fire of his sarcasm, and over whom he flashes the levin-brand of his denunciation, were to take his warnings in time—they or their seed might yet escape a fatal Ramoth-Gilead.

Why have I alluded to this **man**? I have

alluded to him, reader, because I think I see in him an intellect profounder and more unique than his contemporaries have yet recognized; because I regard him as the first social regenerator of the day—as the very master of that working corps who would restore to rectitude the warped system of things.

JAMES ANTHONY FROUDE

Born in 1818, died in 1894; educated at Oxford; Fellow of Exeter in 1842; associated with John Henry Newman in the high church movement; owing to change in his religious views, took up literature as a profession; came to the United States in 1872, where he lectured; visited Africa and Australia afterward; made Professor of Modern History at Oxford in 1892 as successor to Freeman; published his "History of England" in 1856-70, "Short Studies on Great Subjects" in 1867-77, "Cæsar" in 1879, "Reminiscences of Carlyle" in 1881, and "Life of Carlyle" in 1882 and following year.

I

OF HISTORY AS A SCIENCE [1]

"WHAT is History," said Napoleon, "but a fiction agreed upon?" "My friend," said Faust to the student, who was growing enthusiastic about the spirit of past ages,—"my friend, the times which are gone are a book with seven seals; and what you call the spirit of past ages is but the spirit of this or that worthy gentleman in whose mind those ages are reflected."

One lesson, and only one, history may be said to repeat with distinctness; that the world is built somehow on moral foundations; that, in the long run, it is well with the good; in the long run it is ill with the wicked. But this is no

[1] From the first chapter in Volume I of the "Short Studies on Great Subjects," the same being a lecture delivered at the Royal Institution in London, November 5, 1864.

science; it is no more than the old doctrine taught long ago by the Hebrew prophets. The theories of M. Comte and his disciples advance us, after all, not a step beyond the trodden and familiar ground. If men are not entirely animals, they are at least half animals, and are subject in this aspect of them to the conditions of animals. So far as those parts of man's doings are concerned, which neither have, nor need have, anything moral about them, so far the laws of him are calculable. There are laws for his digestion, and laws of the means by which his digestive organs are supplied with matter. But pass beyond them, and where are we? In a world where it would be as easy to calculate men's actions by laws like those of positive philosophy as to measure the orbit of Neptune with a foot rule, or weigh Sirius in a grocer's scale.

And it is not difficult to see why this should be. The first principle, on which the theory of a science of history can be plausibly argued, is that all actions whatsoever arise from self-interest. It may be enlightened self-interest, it may be unenlightened; but it is assumed as an axiom that every man, in whatever he does, is aiming at something which he considers will promote his happiness. His conduct is not determined by his will; it is determined by the object of his desire. Adam Smith, in laying the foundations of political economy, expressly eliminates every other motive. He does not say that men never act on other motives; still less, that they never ought to act on other motives. He asserts merely that, as far as the arts of production are concerned and of buying and selling, the action of self-interest may be counted upon as uniform. What Adam Smith says of political economy, Mr. Buckle [2] would extend over the whole circle of human activity.

Now, that which especially distinguishes a high order of man from a low order of man—that which constitutes human goodness, human greatness, human nobleness—is surely not the degree of enlightenment with which men pursue their own advantage; but it is self-forgetfulness; it is self-sacrifice; it is the disregard of personal pleasure, personal indulgence, personal advantages remote or present, because some other line of conduct is more right.

We are sometimes told that this is but another way of expressing the same thing; that, when a man prefers doing what is right, it is only because to do right gives him a higher satisfaction. It appears to me, on the contrary, to be a difference in the very heart and nature of things. The martyr goes to the stake, the patriot to the scaffold, not with a view to any future reward to themselves, but because it is a glory to fling away their lives for truth and freedom. And so through all phases of existence, to the smallest details of common life, the beautiful character is the unselfish character. Those whom we most love and admire are those to whom the thought of self seems never to occur; who do simply and with no ulterior aim—with no thought whether it will be pleasant to themselves or unpleasant —that which is good and right and generous.

Is this still selfishness, only more enlightened? I do not think so. The essence of true nobility

[2] In his "History of Civilization in England."

is neglect of self. Let the thought of self pass in, and the beauty of a great action is gone, like the bloom from a soiled flower. Surely it is a paradox to speak of the self-interest of a martyr who dies for a cause, the triumph of which he will never enjoy; and the greatest of that great company in all ages would have done what they did, had their personal prospects closed with the grave. Nay, there have been those so zealous for some glorious principle as to wish themselves blotted out of the book of Heaven if the cause of Heaven could succeed.

And out of this mysterious quality, whatever it be, arise the higher relations of human life, the higher modes of human obligation. Kant, the philosopher, used to say that there were two things which overwhelmed him with awe as he thought of them. One was the star-sown deep of space, without limit and without end; the other was right and wrong. Right, the sacrifice of self to good; wrong, the sacrifice of good to self,—not graduated objects of desire, to which we are determined by the degrees of our knowledge, but wide asunder as pole and pole, as light and darkness; one, the object of infinite love; the other, the object of infinite detestation and scorn. It is in this marvelous power in men to do wrong (it is an old story, but none the less true for that),—it is in this power to do wrong—wrong or right, as it lies somehow with ourselves to choose—that the impossibility stands of forming scientific calculations of what men will do before the fact, or scientific explanations of what they have done after the fact. If men were consistently selfish, you might analyze their motives; if they were consistently noble, they would express in their conduct the laws of the highest perfection. But so long as two natures are mixt together, and the strange creature which results from the combinations is now under one influence and now under another, so long you will make nothing of him except from the old-fashioned moral—or, if you please, imaginative—point of view.

Even the laws of political economy itself cease to guide us when they touch moral government. So long as labor is a chattel to be bought and sold, so long, like other commodities, it follows the condition of supply and demand. But if, for his misfortune, an employer considers that he stands in human relations to his workmen; if he believes rightly or wrongly, that he is responsible for them; that in return for their labor he is bound to see that their children are decently taught, and they and their families decently fed and clothed and lodged; that he ought to care for them in sickness and in old age,—then political economy will no longer direct him, and the relations between himself and his dependents will have to be arranged on quite other principles.

So long as he considers only his own material profit, so long supply and demand will settle every difficulty; but the introduction of a new factor spoils the equation.

And it is precisely in this debatable ground of low motives and noble emotions; in the struggle, ever failing yet ever renewed, to carry truth and justice into the administration of human society; in the establishment of states and in the overthrow of tyrannies; in the rise and fall of creeds; in the world of ideas; in the character and deeds of the great actors in the drama of life, where good and evil fight out their everlasting battle, now ranged in opposite camps, now and more often in the heart, both of them, of each living man,—that the true human interest of history resides. The progress of industries, the growth of material and mechanical civilization, are interesting; but they are not the most interesting. They have their reward in the increase of material comforts; but, unless we are mistaken about our nature, they do not highly concern us after all.

Once more; not only is there in men this baffling duality of principle, but there is something else in us which still more defies scientific analysis.

Mr. Buckle would deliver himself from the eccentricities of this and that individual by a doctrine of averages. Tho he can not tell whether A, B, or C will cut his throat, he may assure himself that one man in every fifty thousand, or thereabout (I forget the exact proportion), will cut his throat, and with this he consoles himself. No doubt it is a comforting discovery. Unfortunately, the average of one generation need not be the average of the next. We may be converted by the Japanese, for all that we know, and the Japanese methods of taking leave of life may become fashionable among us. Nay, did not Novalis suggest that the whole race of men would at last become so disgusted with their impotence, that they would extinguish themselves by a simultaneous act of suicide, and make room for a better order of things? Anyhow, the fountain out of which the race is flowing perpetually changes; no two generations are alike. Whether there is a change in the organization itself we can not tell; but this is certain,—that, as the planet varies with the atmosphere which surrounds it, so each new generation varies from the last, because it inhales as its atmosphere the accumulated experience and knowledge of the whole past of the world. These things form the spiritual air which we breathe as we grow; and, in the infinite multiplicity of elements of which that air is now composed, it is forever matter of conjecture what the minds will be like which expand under its influence.

From the England of Fielding and Richardson to the England of Miss Austen, from the England of Miss Austen to the England of railways and free trade, how vast the change! Yet perhaps Sir Charles Grandison would not seem so strange to us now as one of ourselves will seem to our great-grandchildren. The world moves faster and faster; and the difference will probably be considerably greater.

The temper of each new generation is a continual surprize. The Fates delight to contradict our most confident expectations. Gibbon believed that the era of conquerors was at an end. Had he lived out the full life of man, he would have seen Europe at the feet of Napoleon. But a few years ago we believed the world had grown too civilized for war, and the Crystal Palace in Hyde Park was to be the inauguration of a new era. Battles bloody as Napoleon's are now the familiar tale of every day; and the arts which have made greatest progress are the arts of destruction. What next? We may strain our eyes into the future which lies beyond this waning century; but never was conjecture more at fault. It is blank darkness, which even the imagination fails to people.

What, then, is the use of history, and what are its lessons? If it can tell us little of the past, and nothing of the future, why waste our time over so barren a study?

First, it is a voice forever sounding across the centuries the laws of right and wrong. Opinions alter, manners change, creeds rise and fall, but the moral law is written on the tablets of eternity. For every false word or unrighteous deed, for cruelty and oppression, for lust or vanity, the price has to be paid at last, not always by the chief offenders, but paid by some one. Justice and truth alone endure and live. Injustice and falsehood may be long-lived, but doomsday comes at last to them, in French revolutions and other terrible ways.

That is one lesson of history. Another is, that we should draw no horoscope; that we should expect little, for what we expect will not come to pass. Revolutions, reformations,—those vast movements into which heroes and saints have flung themselves, in the belief that they were the dawn of the millenium,—have not borne the fruit which they looked for. Millenniums are still far away. These great convulsions leave the world changed,—perhaps improved, but not improved as the actors in them hoped it would be. Luther would have gone to work with less heart could he have foreseen the Thirty Years' War, and in the distance the theology of Tübingen. Washington might have hesitated to draw the sword against England, could he have seen the country which he made as we see it now. [3]

The most reasonable anticipations fail us, antecedents the most opposite mislead us, because the conditions of human problems never repeat themselves. Some new feature alters everything —some element which we detect only in its after-operation.

Bishop Butler says somewhere that the best book which could be written would be a book consisting only of premises, from which the readers should draw conclusions for themselves. The highest poetry is the very thing which Butler requires, and the highest history ought to be. We should no more ask for a theory of this or that period of history, than we should ask for a theory of "Macbeth" or "Hamlet." Philosophies of history, sciences of history,—all these there will continue to be; the fashions of them will change, as our habits of thought will change; each new philosopher will find his chief employment in showing that before him no one understood anything; but the drama of history is imperishable, and the lessons of it will be like what we learn from Homer or Shakespeare,— lessons for which we have no words.

The address of history is less to the understanding than to the higher emotions. We learn in it to sympathize with what is great and good; we learn to hate what is base. In the anomalies of fortune we feel the mystery of our mortal

[3] This is a reference to the condition of this country during the Civil War.

existence; and in the companionship of the illustrious natures who have shaped the fortunes of the world, we escape from the littlenesses which cling to the round of common life, and our minds are tuned in a higher and nobler key.

For the rest, and for those large questions which I touched in connection with Mr. Buckle, we live in times of disintegration, and none can tell what will be after us. What opinions, what convictions, the infant of to-day will find prevailing on the earth, if he and it live out together to the middle of another century, only a very bold man would undertake to conjecture. "The time will come," said Lichtenberg, in scorn at the materializing tendencies of modern thought, —"the time will come when the belief in God will be as the tales with which old women frighten children; when the world will be a machine, the ether a gas, and God will be a force." Mankind, if they last long enough on the earth, may develop strange things out of themselves; and the growth of what is called the Positive Philosophy is a curious commentary on Lichtenberg's prophecy. But whether the end be seventy years hence, or seven hundred,—be the close of the mortal history of humanity as far distant in the future as its shadowy beginnings seem now to lie behind us,—this only we may foretell with confidence,—that the riddle of man's nature will remain unsolved. There will be that in him yet which physical laws will fail to explain,—that something, whatever it be, in himself and in the world, which science can not fathom, and which suggests the unknown possibilities of his origin and his destiny.

II

THE CHARACTER OF HENRY VIII [4]

PROTESTANTS and Catholics united to condemn a government under which both had suffered; and a point on which enemies were agreed was assumed to be proved. When I commenced the examination of the records, I brought with me the inherited impression, from which I had neither any thought nor any expectation that I should be disabused. I found that it melted between my hands, and with it disappeared that other fact, so difficult to credit, yet as it had appeared so impossible to deny, that English Parliaments, English judges, English clergy, statesmen whose beneficent legislation survives among the most valued of our institutions, prelates who were the founders and martyrs of the English Church, were the cowardly accomplices of abominable atrocities, and had disgraced themselves with a sycophancy which the Roman senate imperfectly approached when it fawned on Nero.

Henry had many faults. They have been exhibited in the progress of the narrative: I need not return to them. But his position was one of unexampled difficulty; and by the work which he accomplished, and the conditions, internal and external, under which his task was allotted to him, he, like every other man, ought to be judged. He was inconsistent: he can bear the reproach of it. He ended by accepting and approving what

[4] From the "History of England."

he had commenced with persecuting; yet it was with the honest inconsistency which distinguishes the conduct of most men of practical ability in times of change, and even by virtue of which they obtain their success. If at the commencement of the movement he had regarded the eucharist as a "remembrance," he must either have concealed his convictions or he would have forfeited his throne; if he had been a stationary bigot, the Reformation might have waited for a century, and would have been conquered only by an internecine war.

But as the nation moved the King moved, leading it, but not outrunning it; checking those who went too fast, dragging forward those who lagged behind. The conservatives, all that was sound and good among them, trusted him because he so long continued to share their conservatism; when he threw it aside he was not reproached with breach of confidence, because his own advance had accompanied theirs.

Protestants have exclaimed against the Six Articles bill; Romanists against the Act of Supremacy. Philosophers complain that the prejudices of the people were needlessly violated, that opinions should have been allowed to be free, and the reform of religion have been left to be accomplished by reason. Yet, however cruel was the Six Articles bill, the governing classes even among the laity were unanimous in its favor. The King was not converted by a sudden miracle; he believed the traditions in which he had been trained; his eyes, like the eyes of others, opened but slowly; and unquestionably, had he conquered for himself in their fulness the modern principles of toleration, he could not have governed by them a nation which was itself intolerant. Perhaps, of all living Englishmen who shared Henry's faith, there was not one so little desirous as himself of enforcing it by violence. His personal exertions were ever to mitigate the action of the law, while its letter was sustained; and England at its worst was a harbor of refuge to the Protestants, compared to the Netherlands, to France, to Spain, or even to Scotland.

That the Romanists should have regarded him as a tyrant is natural; and were it true that English subjects owed fealty to the Pope, their feeling was just. But however desirable it may be to leave religious opinions unfettered, it is certain that if England was legitimately free, she could tolerate no difference of opinion on a question of allegiance, so long as Europe was conspiring to bring her back into slavery. So long as the English Romanists refused to admit without mental reservation that, if foreign enemies invaded this country in the Pope's name, their place must be at the side of their own sovereign, "religion" might palliate the moral guilt of their treason, but it could not exempt them from its punishment.

But these matters have been discust in the details of this history, where alone they can be understood.

Beyond and besides the Reformation, the constitution of these islands now rests in large measure on foundations laid in this reign. Henry brought Ireland within the reach of English civilization. He absorbed Wales and the Palatinates into the general English system. He it was who raised the House of Commons from the narrow duty of voting supplies, and of passing without discussion the measures of the Privy Council, and converted them into the first power in the State under the Crown. When he ascended the throne, so little did the Commons care for their privileges that their attendance at the sessions of Parliament was enforced by a law. They woke into life in 1529, and they became the right hand of the King to subdue the resistance of the House of Lords, and to force upon them a course of legislation which from their hearts they detested. Other kings in times of difficulty summoned their ''great councils,'' composed of peers, or prelates, or municipal officials, or any persons whom they pleased to nominate. Henry VIII broke through the ancient practise, and ever threw himself on the representatives of the people. By the Reformation and by the power which he forced upon them he had so interwoven the House of Commons with the highest business of the state that the peers thenceforward sunk to be their shadow.

Something, too, ought to be said of his individual exertions in the details of state administration. In his earlier life, tho active and assiduous, he found leisure for elegant accomplishments, for splendid amusements, for relaxations careless, extravagant, sometimes questionable. As his life drew onward, his lighter tastes disappeared, and the whole energy of his intellect was prest into the business of the commonwealth. Those who have examined the printed state papers may form some impression of his industry from the documents which are his own composition, and the letters which he wrote and received; but only persons who have seen the original manuscripts, who have observed the traces of his pen in side-notes and corrections, and the handwritings of his secretaries in diplomatic commissions, in drafts of Acts of Parliament, in expositions and formularies, in articles of faith, in proclamations, in the countless multitude of documents of all sorts, secular or ecclesiastical, which contain the real history of this extraordinary reign—only they can realize the extent of labor to which he sacrificed himself, and which brought his life to a premature close. His personal faults were great, and he shared, besides them, in the errors of his age; but far deeper blemishes would be but as scars upon the features of a sovereign who in trying times sustained nobly the honor of the English name, and carried the commonwealth securely through the hardest crisis in its history.

III

CÆSAR'S MISSION [5]

THERE is a legend that at the death of Charles V the accusing angel appeared in heaven with a catalog of deeds which no advocate could palliate—countries laid desolate, cities sacked and burned, lists of hundreds of thousands of widows and children brought to misery by the political ambition of a single man. The evil spirit de-

[5] From the concluding chapter of "Cæsar—A Sketch."

manded the offender's soul, and it seemed as if mercy itself could not refuse him the award. But at the last moment the Supreme Judge interfered. The emperor, He said, had been sent into the world at a peculiar time, for a peculiar purpose, and was not to be tried by the ordinary rules. Titian has painted the scene: Charles kneeling before the throne, with the consciousness, as became him, of human infirmities written upon his countenance, yet neither afraid nor abject, relying in absolute faith that the Judge of all mankind would do right.

Of Cæsar too it may be said that he came into the world at a special time and for a special object. The old religions were dead, from the Pillars of Hercules to the Euphrates and the Nile, and the principles on which human society had been constructed were dead also. There remained of spiritual conviction only the common and human sense of justice and morality; and out of this sense some ordered system of government had to be constructed, under which quiet men could live and labor and eat the fruit of their industry. Under a rule of this material kind there can be no enthusiasm, no chivalry, no saintly aspirations, no patriotism of the heroic type. It was not to last forever. A new life was about to dawn for mankind. Poetry, and faith, and devotion were to spring again out of the seeds which were sleeping in the heart of humanity.

But the life which is to endure grows slowly; and as the soil must be prepared before the wheat can be sown, so before the kingdom of heaven could throw up its shoots there was needed a kingdom of this world where the nations were neither torn in pieces by violence nor were rushing after false ideals and spurious ambitions. Such a kingdom was the empire of the Cæsars—a kingdom where peaceful men could work, think, and speak as they pleased, and travel freely among provinces ruled for the most part by Gallios who protected life and property, and forbade fanatics to tear each other in pieces for their religious opinions. "It is not lawful for us to put any man to death," was the complaint of the Jewish priests to the Roman governor. Had Europe and Asia been covered with independent nations, each with a local religion represented in its ruling powers, Christianity must have been stifled in its cradle. If St. Paul had escaped the Sanhedrim at Jerusalem, he would have been torn to pieces by the silversmiths at Ephesus. The appeal to Cæsar's judgment-seat was the shield of his mission, and alone made possible his success.

And this spirit, which confined government to its simple duties, while it left opinion unfettered, was especially present in Julius Cæsar himself. From cant of all kinds he was totally free. He was a friend of the people, but he indulged in no enthusiasm for liberty. He never dilated on the beauties of virtue, or complimented, as Cicero did, a Providence in which he did not believe. He was too sincere to stoop to unreality. He held to the facts of this life and to his own convictions; and as he found no reason for supposing that there was a life beyond the grave he did not pretend to expect it. He respected the religion of the Roman state as an institution established by the laws. He encouraged or left unmolested the creeds and practises of the uncounted sects or tribes who were gathered under the eagles. But his own writings contain nothing to indicate that he himself had any religious belief at all. He saw no evidence that the gods practically interfered in human affairs. He never pretended that Jupiter was on his side. He thanked his soldiers after a victory, but he did not order Te Deums to be sung for it; and in the absence of these conventionalisms he perhaps showed more real reverence than he could have displayed by the freest use of the formulas of pietism.

He fought his battles to establish some tolerable degree of justice in the government of this world; and he succeeded, tho he was murdered for doing it.

Strange and startling resemblance between the fate of the founder of the kingdom of this world and of the Founder of the kingdom not of this world for which the first was a preparation. Each was denounced for making himself a king. Each was maligned as the friend of publicans and sinners; each was betrayed by those whom he had loved and cared for; each was put to death; and Cæsar also was believed to have risen again and ascended into heaven and become a divine being.

JOHN RUSKIN

Born in 1819, died in 1900; his father a wealthy wine-merchant in London; educated at Oxford; published the first volume of "Modern Painters" in 1843; made professor at Cambridge in 1858; professor at Oxford in 1869; retired to his estate on Coniston Lake in 1855; published "Lamps of Architecture" in 1849, "Stones of Venice" in 1851-53, followed by a large number of other works, including his "Autobiography" in 1887-88.

I

OF THE HISTORY AND SOVEREIGNTY OF VENICE[1]

SINCE first the dominion of men was asserted over the ocean, three thrones, of mark beyond all other, have been set upon its sands; the thrones of Tyre, Venice and England. Of the first of these great powers only the memory remains; of the second, the ruin; the third, which inherits their greatness, if it forget their example, may be led through prouder eminence to less pitied destruction.

The exaltation, the sin, and the punishment of Tyre have been recorded for us, in perhaps the most touching words ever uttered by the prophets of Israel against the cities of the stranger. But we read them as a lovely song; and close our ears to the sternness of their warning; for the very depth of the fall of Tyre has blinded us to its reality, and we forget, as we watch the

[1] From Chapter I of "The Stones of Venice."

bleaching of the rocks between the sunshine and the sea, that they were once "as in Eden, the garden of God."

Her successor, like her in perfection of beauty, tho less in endurance of dominion, is still left for our beholding in the final period of her decline: a ghost upon the sands of the sea, so weak—so quiet—so bereft of all but her loveliness, that we might well doubt, as we watched her faint reflection in the mirage of the lagoon, which was city and which the shadow.

I would endeavor to trace the lines of this image before it be forever lost and to record, as far as I may, the warning which seems to me to be uttered by every one of the fast-gaining waves that beat like passing bells against the stones of Venice.

It would be difficult to overrate the value of the lessons which might be derived from a faithful study of the history of this strange and mighty city; a history which, in spite of the labor of countless chroniclers, remains in vague and disputable outline—barred with brightness and shade, like the far-away edge of her own ocean, where the surf and the sand-banks are mingled with the sky. . . .

Venice is usually conceived as an oligarchy: She was so during a period less than the half of her existence, and that including the days of her decline; and it is one of the first questions needing severe examination, whether that decline was owing in anywise to the change in the form of her government, or altogether, as assuredly in great part, to changes in the character of the persons of whom it was composed.

The state of Venice existed thirteen hundred and seventy-six years, from the first establishment of a consular government on the island of the Rialto to the moment when the general-in-chief of the French army of Italy[2] pronounced the Venetian republic a thing of the past. Of this period, two hundred and seventy-six years were passed in a nominal subjection to the cities of old Venetia, especially to Padua, and in an agitated form of democracy of which the executive appears to have been entrusted to tribunes, chosen one by the inhabitants of each of the principal islands. For six hundred years, during which the power of Venice was continually on the increase, her government was an elective monarchy, her king or doge possessing, in early times at least, as much independent authority as any other European sovereign, but an authority gradually subjected to limitation, and shortened almost daily of its prerogatives, while it increased in a spectral and incapable magnificence. The final government of the nobles, under the image of a king, lasted for five hundred years, during which Venice reaped the fruits of her former energies, consumed them—and expired.

Let the reader therefore conceive the existence of the Venetian state as broadly divided into two periods: the first of nine hundred, the second of five hundred years, the separation being marked by what was called the "Serrar del Consiglio"; that is to say, the final and absolute distinction of the nobles from the commonalty, and the establishment of the government in their hands to the exclusion alike of the influence of

[2] Napoleon Bonaparte.

the people on the one side, and the authority of the doge on the other.

Then the first period, of nine hundred years, presents us with the most interesting spectacle of a people struggling out of anarchy into order and power; and then governed, for the most part, by the worthiest and noblest man whom they could find among them, called their Doge or Leader, with an aristocracy gradually and resolutely forming itself around him, out of which, and at last by which, he was chosen; an aristocracy owing its origin to the accidental numbers, influence, and wealth of some among the families of the fugitives from the older Venetia, and gradually organizing itself, by its unity and heroism, into a separate body.

This first period includes the rise of Venice, her noblest achievements, and the circumstances which determined her character and position among European powers; and within its range, as might have been anticipated, we find the names of all her hero princes—of Pietro Urseolo, Ordalafo Falier, Domenico Michieli, Sebastiano Ziani, and Enrico Dandolo.

The second period opens with a hundred and twenty years, the most eventful in the career of Venice—the central struggle of her life—stained with her darkest crime, the murder of Carrara—disturbed by her most dangerous internal sedition, the conspiracy of Falier—opprest by her most fatal war, the war of Chiozza—and distinguished by the glory of her two noblest citizens (for in this period the heroism of her citizens replaces that of her monarchs), Vittor Pisani and Carlo Zeno.

I date the commencement of the fall of Venice from the death of Carlo Zeno, 8th May, 1418; the visible commencement from that of another of her noblest and wisest children, the Doge Tomaso Mocenigo, who expired five years later. The reign of Foscari followed, gloomy with pestilence and war; a war in which large acquisitions of territory were made by subtle or fortunate policy in Lombardy, and disgrace, significant as irreparable, sustained in the battles on the Po at Cremona, and in the marshes of Caravaggio. In 1454, Venice, the first of the states of Christendom, humiliated herself to the Turk; in the same year was established the Inquisition of State, and from this period her government takes the perfidious and mysterious form under which it is usually conceived. In 1477, the great Turkish invasion spread terror to the shores of the lagoons; and in 1508 the league of Cambrai marks the period usually assigned as the commencement of the decline of the Venetian power; the commercial prosperity of Venice in the close of the fifteenth century blinding her historians to the previous evidence of the diminution of her internal strength. . . .

Throughout her career the victories of Venice, and, at many periods of it, her safety, were purchased by individual heroism; and the man who exalted or saved her was sometimes (oftenest) her king, sometimes a noble, sometimes a citizen. To him no matter nor to her; the real question is not so much what names they bore, or with what powers they were entrusted, as how they were trained; how they were made masters of themselves, servants of their country, patient of distress, impatient of dishonor; and what was the true reason of the change from the time when she could find saviors among those whom she had cast into prison to that when the voices of her own children commanded her to sign covenant with death. . . .

The most curious phenomenon in all Venetian history is the vitality of religion in private life and its deadness in public policy. Amidst the enthusiasm, chivalry, or fanaticism of the other states of Europe, Venice stands, from first to last, like a masked statue; her coldness impenetrable, her exertion only aroused by the touch of a secret spring. That spring was her commercial interest—this the one motive of all her important political acts, or enduring national animosities. She could forgive insults to her honor, but never rivalship in her commerce; she calculated the glory of her conquests by their value, and estimated their justice by their facility. The fame of success remains when the motives of attempts are forgotten; and the casual reader of her history may perhaps be surprized to be reminded that the expedition which was commanded by the noblest of her princes, and whose results added most to her military glory, was one in which, while all Europe around her was wasted by the fire of its devotion, she first calculated the highest price she could exact from its piety for the armament she furnished, and then, for the advancement of her own private interests, at once broke her faith and betrayed her religion. . . .

There are, therefore, two strange and solemn lights in which we have to regard almost every scene in the fitful history of the Rivo Alto. We find, on the one hand, a deep and constant tone of individual religion characterizing the lives of the citizens of Venice in her greatness; we find this spirit influencing them in all the familiar and immediate concerns of life, giving a peculiar dignity to the conduct even of their commercial transactions, and confest by them with a simplicity of faith that may well put to shame the hesitation with which a man of the world at present admits (even if it be so in reality) that religious feeling has any influence over the minor branches of his conduct. And we find as the natural consequence of all this, a healthy serenity of mind and energy of will exprest in all their actions, and a habit of heroism which never fails them, even when the immediate motive of action ceases to be praiseworthy. With the fulness of this spirit the prosperity of the state is exactly correspondent, and with its failure her decline. . . .

I have said that the two orders, Doric and Corinthian, are the roots of all European architecture. You have, perhaps, heard of five orders: but there are only two real orders; and there never can be any more until doomsday. On one of these orders the ornament is convex: those are Doric, Norman, and what else you recollect of the kind. On the other the ornament is concave: those are Corinthian, Early English, Decorated, and what else you recollect of that kind. The transitional form, in which the ornamental line is straight, is the center or root of both. All other orders are varieties of these, or fantasms and grotesques, altogether indefinite in number and species.

This Greek architecture, then, with its two orders, was clumsily copied and varied by the Romans with no particular result, until they began to bring the arch into extensive practical service; except only that the Doric capital was spoiled in endeavors to mend it, and the Corinthian much varied and enriched with fanciful, and often very beautiful imagery. And in this state of things came Christianity: seized upon the arch as her own; decorated it, and delighted in it: invented a new Doric capital to replace the spoiled Roman one: and all over the Roman Empire set to work, with such materials as were nearest at hand, to express and adorn herself as best she could. This Roman Christian architecture is the exact expression of the Christianity of the time, very fervid and beautiful—but very imperfect; in many respects ignorant, and yet radiant with a strong, childlike light of imagination, which flames up under Constantine, illumines all the shores of the Bosporus and the Ægean and the Adriatic Sea, and then gradually, as the people give themselves up to idolatry, becomes corpse-like. The architecture sinks into a settled form—a strange, gilded, and embalmed repose: it, with the religion it exprest; and so would have remained forever—so *does* remain where its languor has been undisturbed. But rough wakening was ordained for it.

The Christian art of the declining empire is divided into two great branches, western and eastern; one centered at Rome, the other at Byzantium, of which the one is the early Christian Romanesque, properly so called, and the other, carried to higher imaginative perfection by Greek workmen, is distinguished from it as Byzantine. But I wish the reader, for the present, to class these two branches of art together in his mind, they being, in points of main importance, the same; that is to say, both of them a true continuance and sequence of the art of old Rome itself, flowing uninterruptedly down from the fountain-head, and entrusted always to the best workmen who could be found—Latins in Italy and Greeks in Greece; and thus both branches may be ranged under the general term of Christian Romanesque, an architecture which had lost the refinement of pagan art in the degradation of the empire, but which was elevated by Christianity to higher aims, and by the fancy of the Greek workmen endowed with brighter forms. And this art the reader may conceive as extending in its various branches over all the central provinces of the empire, taking aspects more or less refined, according to its proximity to the seats of government; dependent for all its power on the vigor and freshness of the religion which animated it; and as that vigor and purity departed, losing its own vitality, and sinking into nerveless rest, not deprived of its beauty, but benumbed, and incapable of advance or change.

Meantime there had been preparation for its renewal. While in Rome and Constantinople, and in the districts under their immediate influence, this Roman art of pure descent was practised in all its refinement, an impure form of it—a patois of Romanesque—was carried by inferior workmen into distant provinces; and still ruder imitations of this patois were executed by the

barbarous nations on the skirts of the empire.
But these barbarous nations were in the strength
of their youth; and while, in the center of Europe, a refined and purely descended art was
sinking into graceful formalism, on its confines
a barbarous and borrowed art was organizing
itself into strength and consistency. The reader
must therefore consider the history of the work
of the period as broadly divided into two great
heads; the one embracing the elaborately languid
succession of the Christian art of Rome; and the
other the imitations of it executed by nations
in every conceivable phase of early organization,
on the edges of the empire, or included in its
now merely nominal extent.

Some of the barbaric nations were, of course,
not susceptible of this influence; and, when they
burst over the Alps, appear, like the Huns, as
scourges only, or mix, as the Ostrogoths, with the
enervated Italians, and give physical strength
to the mass with which they mingle, without
materially affecting its intellectual character. But
others, both south and north of the empire, had
felt its influence, back to the beach of the Indian
Ocean on the one hand, and to the ice creeks
of the North Sea on the other. On the north and
west the influence was of the Latins; on the
south and east, of the Greeks. Two nations, preeminent above all the rest, represent to us the
force of derived mind on either side. As the
central power is eclipsed, the orbs of reflected
light gather into their fulness; and when sen-
suality and idolatry had done their work, and
the religion of the empire was laid asleep in a
glittering sepulcher, the living light rose upon

both horizons, and the fierce swords of the Lombard and Arab were shaken over its golden paralysis.

The work of the Lombard was to give hardihood and system to the enervated body and enfeebled mind of Christendom; that of the Arab was to punish idolatry, and to proclaim the spirituality of worship. The Lombard covered every church which he built with the sculptured representations of bodily exercises—hunting and war. The Arab banished all imagination of creature form from his temples, and proclaimed from their minarets "There is no god but God." Opposite in their character and mission, alike in their magnificence of energy, they came from the North and from the South, the glacier torrent and the lava stream; they met and contended over the wreck of the Roman empire; and the very center of the struggle, the point of pause of both, the dead water of the opposite eddies, charged with embayed fragments of the Roman wreck, is Venice.

The ducal palace of Venice contains the three elements in exactly equal proportions—the Roman, Lombard, and Arab. It is the central building of the world.

II

ST. MARK'S AT VENICE [3]

BEYOND those troops of ordered arches there rises a vision out of the earth, and all the great square seems to have opened from it in a kind of awe, that we may see it far away; a multitude of pillars and white domes, clustered into a long low pyramid of colored light; a treasure heap, it seems, partly of gold and partly of opal and mother-of-pearl, hollowed beneath into five great vaulted porches, ceiled with fair mosaic and beset with sculpture of alabaster, clear as amber and delicate as ivory—sculpture fantastic and involved, of palm-leaves and lilies, and grapes and pomegranates, and birds clinging and fluttering among the branches, all twined together into an endless network of buds and plumes; and in the midst of it the solemn forms of angels, sceptered, and robed to the feet, and leaning to each other across the gates, their figures indistinct among the gleaming of the golden ground through the leaves beside them—interrupted and dim, like the morning light as it faded back among the branches of Eden when first its gates were angel-guarded long ago.

And round the walls of the porches there are set pillars of variegated stones—jasper and porphyry and deep-green serpentine spotted with flakes of snow, and marbles that half refuse and half yield to the sunshine, Cleopatra-like, "their

[3] From "The Stones of Venice," Vol. II.

THE BEST OF THE WORLD'S CLASSICS

bluest veins to kiss''—the shadow, as it steals
back from them, revealing line after line of azure
undulation, as a receding tide leaves the waved
sand; their capitals rich with interwoven tracery,
rooted knots of herbage, and drifting leaves of
acanthus and vine, and mystical signs, all beginning and ending in the Cross; and above them,
in the broad archivolts, a continuous chain of
language and of life—angels, and the signs of
heaven, and the labors of men, each in its appointed season upon the earth; and above these,
another range of glittering pinnacles, mixt with
white arches edged with scarlet flowers—a confusion of delight, amidst which the breasts of
the Greek horses are seen blazing in their breadth
of golden strength, and the St. Mark's Lion,
lifted on a blue field covered with stars: until
at last, as if in ecstasy, the crests of the arches
break into a marble foam, and toss themselves far
into the blue sky in flashes and wreaths of sculptured spray, as if the breakers on the Lido shore
had been frost-bound before they fell, and the
sea-nymphs had inlaid them with coral and ame-
thyst.

Between that grim cathedral of England and
this, what an interval! There is a type of it
in the very birds that haunt them; for instead
of the restless crowd, hoarse-voiced and sable-
winged, drifting on the bleak upper air, the St.
Mark's porches are full of doves, that nestle
among the marble foliage, and mingle the soft
iridescence of their living plumes, changing at
every motion, with the tints, hardly less lovely,
that have stood unchanged for seven hundred
years.

And what effect has this splendor on those who pass beneath it? You may walk from sunrise to sunset, to and fro, before the gateway of St. Mark's, and you will not see an eye lifted to it, nor a countenance brightened by it. Priest and layman, soldier and civilian, rich and poor. pass by it alike regardlessly. Up to the very recesses of the porches, the meanest tradesmen of the city push their counters; nay, the foundations of its pillars are themselves the seats, not "of them that sell doves" for sacrifice, but of the venders of toys and caricatures. Round the whole square in front of the church there is almost a continuous line of cafés, where the idle Venetians of the middle classes lounge and read empty journals; in its center the Austrian bands play during the time of vespers their martial music jarring with the organ notes—the march drowning the miserere and the sullen crowd thickening round them—a crowd which if it had its will would stiletto every soldier that pipes to it. And in the recesses of the porches, all day long, knots of men of the lowest classes, unemployed and listless, lie basking in the sun like lizards; and unregarded children—every heavy glance of their young eyes full of desperation and stony depravity and their throats hoarse with cursing—gamble and fight and snarl and sleep, hour after hour, clashing their bruised *centesimi* upon the marble ledges of the church porch. And the images of Christ and his angels look down upon it continually.

That we may not enter the church out of the midst of the horror of this, let us turn aside under the portico which looks toward the sea, and passing round within the two massive pillars brought from St. Jean d'Acre,[4] we shall find the gate of the baptistery: let us enter there. The heavy door closes behind us instantly; and the light and the turbulence of the Piazzetta are together shut out by it.

We are in a low vaulted room; vaulted not with arches, but with small cupolas starred with gold and checkered with gloomy figures: in the center is a bronze font charged with rich bas-reliefs; a small figure of the Baptist standing above it in a single ray of light, that glances across the narrow room, dying as it falls from a window high in the wall—and the first thing that it strikes, and the only thing that it strikes brightly, is a tomb. We hardly know if it be a tomb indeed: for it is like a narrow couch set beside the window, low-roofed and curtained; so that it might seem, but that it has some height above the pavement, to have been drawn toward the window, that the sleeper might be wakened early —only there are two angels who have drawn the curtain back, and are looking down upon him. Let us look also and thank that gentle light that rests upon his forehead forever, and dies away upon his breast.

The face is of a man in middle life, but there are two deep furrows right across the forehead, dividing it like the foundations of a tower; the

[4] More commonly known as Acre, a seaport on the Palestine coast, captured by Crusaders in 1104, by Saladin in 1187, and recaptured by the Crusaders in 1191. It was thenceforth held by the Christians for exactly one hundred years, when it became the last Christian stronghold in Palestine to yield. In 1797 Acre was successfully defended by Sir Sidney Smith against Napoleon.

height of it above is bound by the fillet of the ducal cap. The rest of the features are singularly small and delicate, the lips sharp—perhaps the sharpness of death being added to that of the natural lines; but there is a sweet smile upon them, and a deep serenity upon the whole countenance. The roof of the canopy above has been blue, filled with stars; beneath, in the center of the tomb on which the figure rests, is a seated figure of the Virgin, and the border of it all around is of flowers and soft leaves, growing rich and deep as if in a field in summer.

It is the Doge Andrea Dandolo; a man early great among the great of Venice, and early lost. She chose him for her king in his thirty-sixth year; he died ten years later, leaving behind him that history to which we owe half of what we know of her former fortunes.

Look round at the room in which he lies. The floor of it is of rich mosaic, encompassed by a low seat of red marble; and its walls are of alabaster, but worn and shattered and darkly stained with age, almost a ruin—in places the slabs of marble have fallen away altogether, and the rugged brickwork is seen through the rents: but all beautiful—the ravaging fissures fretting their way among the islands and channeled zones of the alabaster and the time stains on its translucent masses darkened into fields of rich golden brown, like the color of seaweed when the sun strikes on it through deep sea. . . .

Through the heavy door whose bronze network closes the place of his rest, let us enter the church itself. It is lost in still deeper twilight, to which the eye must be accustomed for some moments

before the form of the building can be traced;
and then there opens before us a vast cave, hewn
out into the form of a cross, and divided into
shadowy aisles by many pillars. Round the
domes of its roof the light enters only through
narrow apertures like large stars; and here and
there a ray or two from some far-away casement
wanders into the darkness, and casts a narrow
phosphoric stream upon the waves of marble that
heave and fall in a thousand colors along the
floor. What else there is of light is from torches,
of silver lamps, burning ceaselessly in the recesses
of the chapels: the roof sheeted with gold, and
the polished walls covered with alabaster, give
back at every curve and angle some feeble gleaming to the flames; and the glories round the heads
of the sculptured saints flash out upon us as we
pass them, and sink again into the gloom. Under
foot and over head, a continual succession of
crowded imagery, one picture passing into another, as in a dream; forms beautiful and terrible
mixt together; dragons and serpents, and raven-
ing beasts of prey, and graceful birds that in the
midst of them drink from running fountains and
feed from vases of crystal: the passions and the
pleasures of human life symbolized together, and
the mystery of its redemption; for the mazes of
interwoven lines and changeful pictures lead always at last to the Cross, lifted and carved in
every place and upon every stone; sometimes
with the serpent of eternity wrapt round it, sometimes with doves beneath its arms and sweet
herbage growing forth from its feet; but conspicuous most of all on the great rood that crosses
the church before the altar, raised in bright

blazonry against the shadow of the apse. And altho in the recesses of the aisles and chapels, when the mist of the incense hangs heavily, we may see continually a figure traced in faint lines upon their marble—a woman standing with her eyes raised to heaven, and the inscription above her "Mother of God"—she is not here the presiding deity. It is the Cross that is first seen, and always, burning in the center of the temple; and every dome and hollow of its room has the figure of Christ in the utmost height of it, raised in power, or returning in judgment.

Nor is this interior without effect on the minds of the people. At every hour of the day there are groups collected before the various shrines, and solitary worshipers scattered through the darker places of the church—evidently in prayer both deep and reverent, and for the most part profoundly sorrowful. The devotees at the greater number of the renowned shrines of Romanism may be seen murmuring their appointed prayers with wandering eyes and unengaged gestures: but the step of the stranger does not disturb those who kneel on the pavement of St. Mark's; and hardly a moment passes, from early morning to sunset, in which we may not see some half-veiled figure enter beneath the Arabian porch, cast itself into long abasement on the floor of the temple, and then, rising slowly with more confirmed step, and with a passionate kiss and clasp of the arms given to the feet of the crucifix, by which the lamps burn always in the northern aisle, leave the church as if comforted. . . .

It was in the hearts of the old Venetian people far more than a place of worship. It was at once a type of the redeemed Church of God, and a scroll for the written Word of God. It was to be to them, both an image of the Bride, all glorious within, her clothing of wrought gold; and the actual Table of the Law and the Testimony, written within and without. And whether honored as the Church or as the Bible, was it not fitting that neither the gold nor the crystal should be spared in the adornment of it; that, as the symbol of the Bride, the building of the wall thereof should be of jasper, and the foundations of it garnished with all manner of precious stones; and that, as the channel of the Word, that triumphant utterance of the Psalmist should be true of it—"I have rejoiced in the way of thy testimonies, as much as in all riches?" And shall we not look with changed temper down the long perspective of St. Mark's Place toward the sevenfold gates and glowing domes of its temple, when we know with what solemn purpose the shafts of it were lifted above the pavement of the populous square? Men met there from all countries of the earth, for traffic or for pleasure; but, above the crowd swaying forever to and fro in the restlessness of avarice or thirst of delight, was seen perpetually the glory of the temple, attesting to them, whether they would hear or whether they would forbear, that there was one treasure which the merchantman might buy without a price, and one delight better than all others, in the word and the statutes of God.

III

OF WATER [5]

OF all inorganic substances, acting in their own proper nature, and without assistance or combination, water is the most wonderful. If we think of it as the course of all the changefulness and beauty which we have seen in clouds; then as the instrument by which the earth we have contemplated was modeled into symmetry, and its crags chiseled into grace; then as, in the form of snow, it robes the mountains it has made with that transcendent light which we could not have conceived if we had not seen; then as it exists in the foam of the torrent—in the iris which spans it, in the morning mist which rises from it, in the deep crystalline pools which mirror its hanging shore, in the broad lake and glancing river; finally, in that which is to all human minds the best emblem of unwearied, unconquerable power, the wild, various, fantastic, tameless unity of the sea; what shall we compare to this mighty, this universal element, for glory and for beauty? or how shall we follow its eternal changefulness of feeling: It is like trying to paint a soul.

To suggest the ordinary appearance of calm water—to lay on canvas as much evidence of surface and reflection as may make us understand that water is meant—is, perhaps, the easiest task of art; and even ordinary running or falling

[5] From "Modern Painters," Vol. II, Section V.

water may be sufficiently rendered, by observing careful curves of projection with a dark ground, and breaking a little white over it, as we see done with judgment and truth by Ruysdael. But to paint the actual play of hue on the reflective surface, or to give the forms and fury of water when it begins to show itself—to give the flashing and rocket-like velocity of a noble cataract, or the precision and grace of the sea wave, so exquisitely modeled, tho so mockingly transient —so mountainous in its form, yet so cold-like in its motion—with its variety and delicacy of color, when every ripple and wreath has some peculiar passage of reflection upon itself alone, and the radiating and scintillating sunbeams are mixt with the dim hues of transparent depth and dark rock below;—to do this perfectly is beyond the power of man; to do it even partially, has been granted to but one or two, even of those few who have dared to attempt it. . . .

Now, the fact is, that there is hardly a roadside pond or pool which has not as much landscape *in* it as above it. It is not the brown, muddy, dull thing we suppose it to be; it has a heart like ourselves, and in the bottom of that there are the boughs of the tall trees, and the blades of the shaking grass, and all manner of hues, of variable, pleasant light out of the sky; nay, the ugly gutter, that stagnates over the drain bars, in the heart of the foul city, is not altogether base; down in that, if you will look deep enough, you may see the dark, serious blue of far-off sky, and the passing of pure clouds. It is at your own will that you see in that despised stream, either the refuse of the street, or the image of the sky—

so it is with almost all other things that we unkindly despise. . . .

Stand for half an hour beside the fall of Schaffhausen, on the north side where the rapids are long, and watch how the vault of water first bends, unbroken, in pure, polished velocity, over the arching rocks at the brow of the cataract, covering them with a dome of crystal twenty feet thick—so swift that its motion is unseen except when a foam globe from above darts over it like a falling star; and how the trees are lighted above it under all their leaves, at the instant that it breaks into foam; and how all the hollows of that foam burn with green fire like so much shattering chrysoprase; and how, ever and anon, startling you with its white flash, a jet of spray leaps hissing out of the fall, like a rocket, bursting in the wind and driven away in dust, filling the air with light; and how, through the curdling wreaths of the restless, crashing abyss below, the blue of the water, paled by the foam in its body, shows purer than the sky through white rain-cloud; while the shuddering iris stoops in tremulous stillness over all, fading and flushing alternately through the choking spray and shattered sunshine, hiding itself at last among the thick golden leaves which toss to and fro in sympathy with the wild water; their dripping masses lifted at intervals, like sheaves of loaded corn, by some stronger gush from the cataract and bowed again upon the mossy rocks as its roar dies away; the dew gushing from their thick branches through drooping clusters of emerald herbage, and sparkling in white threads along the dark rocks of the shore, feeding the lichens which chase and checker them with purple and silver. . . .

When water, not in very great body, runs in a rocky bed much interrupted by hollows, so that it can rest every now and then in a pool as it goes along, it does not acquire a continuous velocity of motion. It pauses after every leap, and curdles about, and rests a little, and then goes on again; and if in this comparatively tranquil and rational state of mind it meets with any obstacle, as a rock or stone, it parts on each side of it with a little bubbling foam, and goes round; if it comes to a step in its bed, it leaps it lightly, and then after a little splashing at the bottom, stops again to take breath. But if its bed be on a continuous slope, not much interrupted by hollows, so that it can not rest, or if its own mass be so increased by flood that its usual resting-places are not sufficient for it, but that it is perpetually pushed out of them by the following current, before it has had time to tranquilize itself, it of course gains velocity with every yard that it runs; the impetus got at one leap is carried to the credit of the next, until the whole stream becomes one mass of unchecked, accelerating motion. Now when water in this state comes to an obstacle, it does not part at it but clears it, like a race-horse; and when it comes to a hollow, it does not fill it up and run out leisurely at the other side, but it rushes down into it and comes up again on the other side, as a ship into the hollow of the sea. Hence, the whole appearance of the bed of the stream is changed, and all the lines of the water altered in their nature. The quiet stream is a succession of leaps

and pools; the leaps are light and springy, and
parabolic, and make a great deal of splashing
when they tumble into the pool; then we have
a space of quiet curdling water, and another
similar leap below.

But the stream when it has gained an impetus
takes the shape of its bed, never stops, is equally
deep and equally swift everywhere, goes down
into every hollow, not with a leap, but with a
swing, not foaming, nor splashing, but in the
bending line of a strong sea-wave, and comes up
again on the other side, over rock and ridge,
with the ease of a bounding leopard; if it meet
a rock three or four feet above the level of its
bed, it will neither part nor foam, nor express
any concern about the matter, but clear it in a
smooth dome of water, without apparent exertion, coming down again as smoothly on the other
side; the whole surface of the surge being drawn
into parallel lines by its extreme velocity, but
foamless, except in places where the form of the
bed opposes itself at some direct angle to such
a line of fall, and causes a breaker; so that the
whole river has the appearance of a deep and
raging sea, with this only difference that the
torrent-waves always break backward, and sea-
waves forward. . . .

Few people, comparatively, have ever seen the
effect on the sea of a powerful gale continued
without intermission for three or four days and
nights, and to those who have not I believe it
must be unimaginable, not from the mere force
or size of surge, but from the complete annihila-
tion of the limit between sea and air. The water
from its prolonged agitation is beaten not into

mere creaming foam but into masses of accumulated yeast which hang in ropes and wreaths from wave to wave, and where one curls over to break, form a festoon like a drapery from its edge; these are taken up by the wind, not in dissipating dust, but bodily, in writhing, hanging, coiling masses, which make the air white and thick as with snow, only the flakes are a foot or two long each; the surges themselves are full of foam in their very bodies, underneath, making them white all through, as the water is under a great cataract; and their masses, being thus half water and half air, are torn to pieces by the wind whenever they rise, and carried away in roaring smoke, which chokes and strangles like actual water. Add to this, that when the air has been exhausted of its moisture by long rain, the spray of the sea is caught by it as described above, and covers its surface not merely with the smoke of finely divided water, but with boiling mist; imagine also the low rain-clouds brought down to the very level of the sea, as I have often seen them; whirling and flying in rags and fragments from wave to wave; and finally conceive the surges themselves in their utmost pitch of power, velocity, vastness, and madness, lifting themselves in precipices and peaks, furrowed with their whirl of ascent, through all this chaos; and you will understand that there is indeed no distinction left between the sea and air; that no object, nor horizon, nor any landmark or natural evidence of position is left; that the heaven is all spray, and the ocean all cloud, and that you see no farther than you could see through a cataract. . . .

But, I think, the noblest sea that Turner has ever painted, and, if so, the noblest certainly ever painted by man, is that of the Slave Ship,[c] the chief Academy picture of the Exhibition in 1840. It is a sunset on the Atlantic, after prolonged storm; but the storm is partially lulled, and the torn and streaming rain-clouds are moving in scarlet lines to lose themselves in the hollow of the night. The whole surface of sea included in the picture is divided into two ridges of enormous swell, not high, nor local, but a low, broad heaving of the whole ocean, like the lifting of its bosom by deep drawn breath after the torture of the storm. Between these two ridges the fire of the sunset falls along the trough of the sea, dyeing it with an awful but glorious light, the intense and lurid splendor which burns like gold, and bathes like blood. Along this fiery path and valley, the tossing waves by which the swell of the sea is restlessly divided, lift themselves in dark, indefinite, fantastic forms, each casting a faint and ghastly shadow behind it along the illumined foam. They do not rise everywhere, but three or four together in wild groups, fitfully and furiously, as the under strength of the swell compels or permits them; leaving between them treacherous spaces of level and whirling water, now lighted with green and lamp-like fire, now flashing back the gold of the declining sun, now fearfully dyed from above with the indistinguishable images of the burning

---

[c] Turner's "Slave Ship" was long in Ruskin's possession, if not actually his property. It afterward came to America, and in New York was placed on public exhibition some thirty years ago. It is now in the Museum of Fine Arts in Boston.

clouds, which fall upon them in flakes of crimson and scarlet, and give to the reckless waves the added motion of their own fiery flying. Purple and blue, the lurid shadows of the hollow breakers are cast upon the mist of the night, which gathers cold and low, advancing like the shadow of death upon the guilty ship as it labors amidst the lightning of the sea, its thin masts written upon the sky in lines of blood, girded with condemnation in that fearful hue which signs the sky with horror, and mixes its flaming flood with the sunlight,—and cast far along the desolate heave of the sepulchral waves, incarnadines the multitudinous sea.

I believe, if I were reduced to rest Turner's immortality upon any single work, I should choose this. Its daring conception—ideal in the highest sense of the word—is based on the purest truth, and wrought out with the concentrated knowledge of a life; its color is absolutely perfect, not one false or morbid hue in any part or line, and so modulated that every square inch of canvas is a perfect composition; its drawing as accurate as fearless; the ship buoyant, bending, and full of motion; its tones as true as they are wonderful; and the whole picture dedicated to the most sublime of subjects and impressions—(completing thus the perfect system of all truth, which we have shown to be formed by Turner's works)—the power, majesty, and deathfulness of the open, deep, illimitable sea.

GEORGE ELIOT

Born in 1819, died in 1880; assistant editor of the *Westminster Review* in 1851; lived with George Henry Lewes from 1854 until his death in 1878; married John W. Cross in 1880; translated Strauss's "Life of Jesus" in 1846, published "Scenes of Clerical Life" in 1858, "Adam Bede" in 1859, "Romola" in 1862, "Middlemarch" in 1871, "Daniel Deronda" in 1876.

AT THE HALL FARM [1]

EVIDENTLY that gate is never opened; for the long grass and the great hemlocks grow close against it; and if it were opened, it is so rusty that the force necessary to turn it on its hinges would be likely to pull down the square stone-built pillars, to the detriment of the two stone lionesses which grin with a doubtful carnivorous affability above a coat of arms surmounting each of the pillars. It would be easy enough, by the aid of the nicks in the stone pillars, to climb over the brick wall with its smooth stone coping; but by putting our eyes close to the rusty bars of the gate, we can see the house well enough, and all but the very corners of the grassy inclosure.

It is a very fine old place, of red brick, softened by a pale powdery lichen, which has dispersed itself with happy irregularity, so as to bring the red brick into terms of friendly companionship with the limestone ornaments surrounding the three gables, the windows, and the door-place.

[1] From "Adam Bede."

But the windows are patched with wooden panes, and the door, I think, is like the gate—it is never opened: how it would groan and grate against the stone floor if it were! For it is a solid, heavy, handsome door, and must once have been in the habit of shutting with a sonorous bang behind a liveried lackey who had just seen his master and mistress off the grounds in a carriage and pair.

But at present one might fancy the house in the early stage of a chancery suit, and that the fruit from that grand double row of walnut-trees on the right hand of the inclosure would fall and rot among the grass; if it were not that we heard the booming bark of dogs echoing from great buildings at the back. And now the half-weaned calves that have been sheltering themselves in a gorse-built hovel against the left-hand wall come out and set up a silly answer to that terrible bark, doubtless supposing that it has reference to buckets of milk.

Yes, the house must be inhabited, and we will see by whom; for imagination is a licensed trespasser; it has no fear of dogs, but may climb over walls and peep in at windows with impunity. Put your face to one of the glass panes in the right-hand window: what do you see? A large open fireplace, with rusty dogs in it, and a bare boarded floor; at the far end, fleeces of wool stacked up; in the middle of the floor, some empty corn-bags. That is the furniture of the dining-room. And what through the left-hand window? Several clothes-horses, a pillion, a spinning-wheel, and an old box wide open, and stuffed full of colored rags. At the edge of this box there lies a great wooden doll, which so far as mutilation is concerned bears a strong resemblance to the finest Greek sculpture, and especially in the total loss of its nose. Near it there is a little chair, and the butt-end of a boy's leather long-lasht whip.

The history of the house is plain now. It was once the residence of a country squire, whose family, probably dwindling down to mere spinster-hood, got merged in the more territorial name of Donnithorne. It was once the Hall; it is now the Hall Farm. Like the life in some coast town that was once a watering-place, and is now a port, where the genteel streets are silent and grass-grown, and the docks and warehouses busy and resonant, the life at the Hall has changed its focus, and no longer radiates from the parlor, but from the kitchen and the farm-yard.

Plenty of life there! tho this the drowsiest time of the year, just before hay harvest; and it is the drowsiest time of the day too, for it is close upon three by the sun, and it is half-past three by Mrs. Poyser's handsome eight-day clock. But there is always a stronger sense of life when the sun is brilliant after rain; and now he is pouring down his beams, and making sparkles among the wet straw, and lighting up every patch of vivid green moss on the red tiles of the cow-shed, and turning even the muddy water that is hurrying along the channel to the drain into a mirror for the yellow-billed ducks, who are seizing the opportunity of getting a drink with as much body in it as pos-sible. There is quite a concert of noises: the great bull-dog, chained against the stables, is thrown into furious exasperation by the unwary approach of a cock too near the mouth of his kennel, and sends forth a thundering bark, which is answered by two fox-hounds shut up in the opposite cow-house; the old top-knotted hens, scratching with their chicks among the straw, set up a sympathetic croaking as the discomfited cock joins them; a sow with her brood, all very muddy as to the legs, and curled as to the tail, throws in some deep staccato notes; our friends the calves are bleating from the home croft; and under all, a fine ear discerns the continuous hum of human voices.

For the great barn doors are thrown wide open, and men are busy there mending the harness under the superintendence of Mr. Goby the "whittaw," otherwise saddler, who entertains them with the latest Treddleston gossip. It is certainly rather an unfortunate day that Alick the shepherd has chosen for having the whittaws, since the morning turned out so wet; and Mrs. Poyser has spoken her mind pretty strongly as to the dirt which the extra number of men's shoes brought into the house at dinner-time. Indeed, she has not yet recovered her equanimity on the subject, tho it is now nearly three hours since dinner and the house floor is perfectly clean again; as clean as everything else in that wonderful house-place, where the only chance of collecting a few grains of dust would be to climb on the salt-coffer, and put your finger on the high mantel shelf on which the glittering brass candlesticks are enjoying their summer sinecure; for at this time of year, of course, every one goes to bed while it is yet light, or at least light enough to discern the outline of objects after you have bruised your shins against them. Surely nowhere

else could an oak clock-case and an oak table have
got to such a polish by the hand: genuine "elbow
polish," as Mrs. Poyser called it, for she thanked
God she never had any of your varnished rubbish
in her house. Hetty Sorrel often took the opportunity, when her aunt's back was turned, of looking at the pleasing reflection of herself in those
polished surfaces, for the oak table was usually
turned up like a screen, and was more for ornament than for use; and she could see herself
sometimes in the great round pewter dishes that
were ranged on the shelves above the long deal
dinner-table, or in the hobs of the grate, which
always shone like jasper.

Everything was looking at its brightest at this
moment, for the sun shone right on the pewter
dishes, and from their reflecting surfaces pleasant
jets of light were thrown on mellow oak and
bright brass;—and on a still pleasanter object
than these; for some of the rays fell on Dinah's
finely molded cheek and lit up her pale-red hair
to auburn, as she bent over the heavy household
linen which she was mending for her aunt. No
scene could have been more peaceful, if Mrs.
Poyser, who was ironing a few things that still
remained from the Monday's wash, had not been
making a frequent clinking with her iron, and
moving to and fro whenever she wanted it to cool;
carrying the keen glance of her blue-gray eye
from the kitchen to the dairy, where Hetty was
making up the butter, and from the dairy to the
back kitchen, where Nancy was taking the pies
out of the oven. Do not suppose, however, that
Mrs. Poyser was elderly or shrewish in her appearance; she was a good-looking woman, not

more than eight-and-thirty, of fair complexion and sandy hair, well-shapen, light-footed; the most conspicuous article in her attire was an ample checkered linen apron, which almost covered her skirt; and nothing could be plainer or less noticeable than her cap and gown, for there was no weakness of which she was less tolerant than feminine vanity, and the preference of ornament to utility. The family likeness between her and her niece Dinah Morris, with the contrast between her keenness and Dinah's seraphic gentleness of expression, might have served a painter as an excellent suggestion for a Martha and Mary. Their eyes were just of the same color, but a striking test of the difference in their operation was seen in the demeanor of Trip, the black-and-tan terrier, whenever that much-suspected dog unwarily exposed himself to the freezing arctic ray of Mrs. Poyser's glance. Her tongue was not less keen than her eye, and whenever a damsel came within earshot, seemed to take up an unfinished lecture, as a barrel-organ takes up a tune, precisely at the point where it had left off.

HERBERT SPENCER

Born in 1820, died in 1904; son of a schoolmaster; became
a civil engineer in 1837, but abandoned that calling in 1845;
assistant editor of *The Economist* in 1848-53; published
among many books "The Proper Sphere of Government" in
1842, "Principles of Psychology" in 1855, "Education in
1860, "First Principles" in 1862, and other works in his
"System of Synthetic Philosophy," later; the "Data of
Ethics" in 1879; his "Autobiography" in two volumes appearing in 1905, after his death.

I

THE ORIGIN OF PROFESSIONAL OCCUPATIONS [1]

EGYPT, which, by its records and remains, ex-
hibits so well the early phases of social progress,
shows us how at first various governmental functions, including the professional, were mingled in
the king and in the cluster of those who surrounded the king.

No group of institutions illustrates with greater
clearness the process of social evolution; and none
shows more undeniably how social evolution con-
forms to the law of evolution at large. The germs
out of which the professional agencies arise, forming at first a part of the regulative agency, differentiate from it at the same time that they
differentiate from one another; and while

---

[1] From Volume III of "The Principles of Sociology."
Copyright, 1896, by D. Appleton & Co.

severally being rendered more multiform by the rise of subdivisions, severally become more coherent within themselves and more definitely marked off. The process parallels completely that by which the parts of an individual organism pass from their initial state of simplicity to their ultimate state of complexity.

Originally one who was believed by himself and others to have power over demons—the mystery-man or medicine-man—using coercive methods to expel disease-producing spirits, stood in the place of doctor; and when his appliances, at first supposed to act supernaturally, came to be understood as acting naturally, his office eventually lost its priestly character altogether: the resulting physician class, originally uniform, eventually dividing into distinguishable subclasses while acquiring a definite embodiment.

Less early, because implying more developed groups, arose those who as exhibitors of joy, now in the presence of the living ruler and now in the supposed presence of the deceased ruler, were at first simultaneously singers and dancers, and, becoming specialized from the people at large, presently became distinct from one another; whence, in course of time, two groups of professionals, whose official laudations, political or religious, extended in their range and multiplied in their kinds. And then by like steps were separated from one another vocal and instrumental musicians, and eventually composers; within which classes also there arose subdivisions.

Ovations, now to the living king and now to the dead king, while taking saltatory and musical forms, took also verbal forms, originally spontaneous and irregular, but presently studied and measured; whence, first, the unrhythmical speech of the orator, which under higher emotional excitement grew into the rhythmical speech of the priest poet, chanting verses—verses that finally became established hymns of praise. Meanwhile from accompanying rude imitations of the hero's acts, performed now by one and now by several, grew dramatic representations, which, little by little elaborated, fell under the regulation of a chief actor, who prefigured the playwright. And out of these germs, all pertaining to worship, came eventually the various professions of poets, actors, dramatists, and the subdivisions of these.

The great deeds of the hero god, recited, chanted, or sung, and mimetically rendered, naturally came to be supplemented by details, so growing into accounts of his life; and thus the priest poet gave origin to the biographer, whose narratives, being extended to less sacred personages, became secularized. Stories of the apotheosized chief or king, joined with stories of his companions and amplified by narratives of accompanying transactions, formed the first histories. And from these accounts of the doings of particular men and groups of men, partly true but passing by exaggeration into the mythical, came the wholly mythical, or fiction; which then and always preserved the biographico-historical character. Add to which that out of the criticisms and reflections scattered through this personal literature an impersonal literature slowly emerged; the whole group of these products having as their deepest root the eulogies of the priest poet.

Prompted as were the medicine-men of savages and the priests of early civilized peoples to increase their influence, they were ever stimulated to acquire knowledge of natural actions and the properties of things; and, being in alleged communication with supernatural beings, they were supposed to acquire such knowledge from them. Hence, by implication, the priest became the primitive man of science; and led by his special experiences to speculate about the causes of things, thus entered the sphere of philosophy: both his science and his philosophy being pursued in the service of his religion.

Not only his higher culture, but his alleged intercourse with the gods, whose mouthpiece he was, made him the authority in cases of dispute; and being also, as historian, the authority concerning past transactions and traditional usages, or laws, he acquired in both capacities the character of judge. Moreover, when the growth of legal administration brought the advocate, he, tho usually of lay origin, was sometimes clerical.

Distinguished in early stages as the learned man of the tribe or society, and especially distinguished as the possessor of that knowledge which was thought of most value—knowledge of unseen things—the priest of necessity became the first teacher. Transmitting traditional statements concerning ghosts and gods, at first to neophytes of his class only, but afterward to the cultured classes, he presently, beyond instruction in supernatural things, gave instruction in natural things; and, having been the first secular teacher, has retained a large share in secular teaching even down to our own days.

As making a sacrifice was the original priestly act, and as the building of an altar for the sacrifice was by implication a priestly act, it results that the making of a shelter over the altar, which in its developed form became the temple, was also a priestly act. When the priest, ceasing to be himself the executant, directed the artificers, he continued to be the designer; and when he ceased to be the actual designer, the master builder or architect thereafter continued to fulfil his general directions. And then the temple and the palace in sundry early societies, being at once the residence of the apotheosized ruler and the living ruler (even now a palace usually contains a small temple), and being the first kinds of developed architecture, eventually gave origin to secular architecture.

A rudely carved or modeled image of a man placed on his grave gave origin to the sculptured representation of a god inclosed in his temple. A product of priestly skill at the outset, it continued in some cases to be such among early civilized peoples; and always thereafter, when executed by an artizan, conformed to priestly direction. Extending presently to the representation of other than divine and semidivine personages, it eventually thus passed into its secularized form.

So was it with painting. At first used to complete the carved representation of the revered or worshiped personage, and being otherwise in some tribes used by the priest and his aids for exhibiting the tribal hero's deeds, it long remained subservient to religion, either for the coloring of statues (as it does still in Roman Catholic images of saints, etc.), or for the decoration of temples, or for the portraiture of deceased persons on sarcophagi and stelæ; and when it gained independence it was long employed almost wholly for the rendering of sacred scenes,—its eventual secularization being accompanied by its subdivision into a variety of kinds and of the executant artists into correlative groups.

Thus the process of professional evolution betrays throughout the same traits. In stages like that described by Huc [2] as still existing among the Tibetans, where "the Lama is not merely a priest, he is the painter, poet, sculptor, architect, physician," there are joined in the same individual, or group of individuals, the potentialities out of which gradually arise the specialized groups we know as professions. While out of the one primitive class there come by progressive divergences many classes, each of these classes itself undergoes a kindred change: there are formed in it subdivisions and even sub-subdivisions, which become gradually more marked; so that, throughout, the advance is from an indefinite homogeneity to a definite heterogeneity.

In presence of the fact that the immense majority of mankind adhere pertinaciously to the creeds, political and religious, in which they are brought up; and in presence of the further fact that on behalf of their creeds, however acquired, there are soon enlisted prejudices which practically shut out adverse evidence, it is not to be expected that the foregoing illustrations, even joined with kindred illustrations previously given,

[2] Évariste Régis Huc, a French missionary and traveler in China, born in 1813 and died in 1860. He published several books based on his experiences in Asia.

will make them see that society is a growth and not a manufacture, and has its laws of evolution.

From prime ministers down to plowboys there is either ignorance or disregard of the truth that nations acquire their vital structures by natural processes and not by artificial devices. If the belief is not that social arrangements have been divinely ordered thus or thus, then it is that they have been made thus or thus by kings, or if not by kings, then by parliaments. That they have come about by small accumulated changes not contemplated by rulers is an open secret which only of late has been recognized by a few, and is still unperceived by the many,—educated as well as uneducated. Tho the turning of the land into a food-producing surface, cleared, fenced, drained, and covered with farming appliances, has been achieved by men working for individual profit, not by legislative direction—tho villages, towns, cities, have insensibly grown up under the desires of men to satisfy their wants—tho by spontaneous cooperation of citizens have been formed canals, railways, telegraphs, and other means of communication and distribution, the natural forces which have done all this are ignored as of no account in political thinking.

Our immense manufacturing system with its multitudinous inventions, supplying both home and foreign consumers, and the immense mercantile marine by which its products are taken all over the globe and other products brought back, have been naturally and not artificially originated. That transformation by which, in thousands of years, men's occupations have been so specialized that each, aiding to satisfy some small division of his fellow citizen's needs, has his own needs satisfied by the work of hundreds of others, has taken place without design and unobserved. Knowledge developing into science, which has become so vast in mass that no one can grasp a tithe of it, and which now guides productive activities at large, has resulted from the workings of individuals prompted not by the ruling agency, but by their own inclinations. So, too, has been created the still vaster mass distinguished as literature, yielding the gratifications filling so large a space in our lives. Nor is it otherwise with the literature of the hour. That ubiquitous journalism which provides satisfactions for men's more urgent mental wants has resulted from the activities of citizens severally pursuing private benefits. And supplementing these come the innumerable companies, associations, unions, societies, clubs, subserving enterprise, philanthropy, culture, art, amusement; as well as the multitudinous institutions annually receiving millions by endowments and subscriptions: all of them arising from the unforced cooperations of citizens.

II

SELF-DEPENDENCE AND PATERNALISM [3]

THE enthusiastic philanthropist urgent for some act of parliament to remedy this evil or secure the other good, thinks it a very trivial and far-fetched objection that the people will be morally injured by doing things for them instead of leaving them to do things themselves. He vividly realizes the benefit he hopes to get achieved, which is a positive and readily imaginable thing: he does not realize the diffused, invisible, and slowly accumulating effect wrought on the popular mind, and so does not believe in it; or, if he admits it, thinks it beneath consideration. Would he but remember, however, that all national character is gradually produced by the daily action of circumstances, of which each day's result seems so insignificant as not to be worth mentioning, he would see that what is trifling when viewed in its increments, may be formidable when viewed in its sum total. Or if he would go into the nursery, and watch how repeated actions—each of them apparently unimportant—create, in the end, a habit which will affect the whole future life; he would be reminded that every influence brought to bear on human nature tells, and if continued, tells seriously. The thoughtless mother who hourly yields to the requests: "Mama, tie my pinafore," "Mama, button my shoe," and the

[3] From the "Essays, Moral, Political, and Esthetic." By permission of D. Appleton & Co.

like, can not be persuaded that each of these concessions is detrimental; but the wiser spectator sees that if this policy be long pursued, and be extended to other things, it will end in hopeless dependence. The teacher of the old school who showed his pupil the way out of every difficulty did not perceive that he was generating an attitude of mind greatly militating against success in life. The modern instructor, however, induces his pupil to solve his difficulties himself; believes that in so doing he is preparing him to meet the difficulties which, when he goes into the world, there will be no one to help him through; and finds confirmation for this belief in the fact that a great proportion of the most successful men are self-made.

Well, is it not obvious that this relationship between discipline and success holds good nationally? Are not nations made of men; and are not men subject to the same laws of modification in their adult as in their early years? Is it not true of the drunkard, that each carouse adds a thread to his bonds? of the trader, that each acquisition strengthens the wish for acquisitions? of the pauper, that the more you assist him the more he wants? of the busy man, that the more he has to do the more he can do? And does it not follow that if every individual is subject to this process of adaptation to conditions, a whole nation must be so—that just in proportion as its members are little helped by extraneous power they will become self-helping, and in proportion as they are much helped they will become helpless? What folly is it to ignore these results because they are not direct, and not immediately visible. Tho slowly wrought out, they are inevitable. We can no more elude the laws of human development than we can elude the law of gravitation; and so long as they hold true must these effects occur.

If we are asked in what special directions this alleged helplessness, entailed by much state superintendence, shows itself, we reply that it is seen in a retardation of all social growths requiring self-confidence in the people—in a timidity that fears all difficulties not before encountered—in a thoughtless contentment with things as they are. Let any one, after duly watching the rapid evolution going on in England, where men have been comparatively little helped by governments—or better still, after contemplating the unparalleled progress of the United States, which is peopled by self-made men and the recent descendants of self-made men;—let such a one, we say, go on to the Continent, and consider the relatively slow advance which things are there making; and the still slower advance they would make but for English enterprise.

Let him go to Holland, and see that tho the Dutch early showed themselves good mechanics, and have had abundant practise in hydraulics, Amsterdam has been without any due supply of water until now that works are being established by an English company. Let him go to Berlin, and there be told that, to give that city a water supply such as London has had for generations, the project of an English firm is about to be executed by English capital, under English superintendence. Let him go to Paris, where he will find a similar lack, and a like remedy now under consideration. Let him go to Vienna, and learn that it, in common with other continental cities, is lighted by an English gas company. Let him go on the Rhone, on the Loire, on the Danube, and discover that Englishmen established steam navigation on those rivers. Let him inquire concerning the railways in Italy, Spain, France, Sweden, Denmark, how many of them are English projects, how many have been largely helped by English capital, how many have been executed by English contractors, how many have had English engineers. Let him discover, too, as he will, that where railways have been government made, as in Russia, the energy, the perseverance, and the practical talent developed in England and the United States have been called in to aid.

And then if these illustrations of the progressiveness of a self-dependent race, and the torpidity of paternally governed ones, do not suffice him, he may read Mr. Laing's[4] successive volumes of European travel, and there study the contrast in detail. What, now, is the cause of this contrast? In the order of nature, a capacity for self-help must in every case have been brought into existence by the practise of self-help; and, other things equal, a lack of this capacity must in every case have arisen from the lack of demand for it. Do not these two antecedents and their two consequents agree with the facts as presented in England and Europe? Were not the inhabitants of the two, some centuries ago, much upon a par in point of enterprise? Were not the English even behind, in their manufactures, in their

[4] Samuel Laing traveled in Norway and Sweden in 1834, and published two books recounting his observations.

colonization, and in their commerce? Has not the immense relative change the English have undergone in this respect been coincident with the great relative self-dependence they have been since habituated to? And is not this change proximately ascribable to this habitual self-dependence? Whoever doubts it is asked to assign a more probable cause. Whoever admits it must admit that the enervation of a people by perpetual state aids is not a trifling consideration, but the most weighty consideration. A general arrest of national growth he will see to be an evil greater than any special benefits can compensate for. And, indeed, when, after contemplating this great fact, the overspreading of the earth by the Anglo-Saxons, he remarks the absence of any parallel phenomenon exhibited by a continental race—when he reflects how this difference must depend chiefly on difference of character, and how such difference of character has been mainly produced by difference of discipline; he will perceive that the policy pursued in this matter may have a large share in determining a nation's ultimate fate.

III

THE ORNAMENTAL AND THE USEFUL IN EDUCATION[5]

It has been truly remarked that, in order of time, decoration precedes dress. Among people who submit to great physical suffering that they may have themselves handsomely tattooed, extremes of temperature are borne with but little attempt at mitigation. Humboldt tells us that an Orinoco Indian, tho quite regardless of bodily comfort, will yet labor for a fortnight to purchase pigment wherewith to make himself admired; and that the same woman who would not hesitate to leave her hut without a fragment of clothing on, would not dare to commit such a breach of decorum as to go out unpainted. Voyagers uniformly find that colored beads and trinkets are much more prized by wild tribes than are calicoes or broadcloths. And the anecdotes we have of the ways in which, when shirts and coats are given, they turn them to some ludicrous display, show how completely the idea of ornament predominates over that of use. Nay, there are still more extreme illustrations: witness the fact narrated by Captain Speke[6] of his African attend-

[5] From "Education, Intellectual, Moral and Physical." By permission of D. Appleton & Co.

[6] John H. Speke, who, in company with Sir Richard Burton, visited the lakes of Central Africa in 1850, and crossed the continent, discovering the Victoria Nyanza and the main source of the Nile in 1860-63.

ants, who strutted about in their goatskin mantles
when the weather was fine, but when it was wet,
took them off, folded them up, and went about
naked, shivering in the rain! Indeed, the facts
of aboriginal life seem to indicate that dress is
developed out of decorations. And when we remember that even among ourselves most think
more about the fineness of the fabric than its
warmth, and more about the cut than the convenience—when we see that the function is still
in great measure subordinated to the appearance,
we have further reason for inferring such an
origin.

It is not a little curious that the like relations
hold with the mind. Among mental as among
bodily acquisitions, the ornamental comes before
the useful. Not only in times past, but almost
as much in our own era, that knowledge which
conduces to personal well-being has been post-
poned to that which brings applause. In the Greek
schools, music, poetry, rhetoric, and a philosophy
which, until Socrates taught, had but little bearing upon action, were the dominant subjects;
while knowledge, aiding the arts of life, had a
very subordinate place. And in our own universities and schools at the present moment the
like antithesis holds. We are guilty of something
like a platitude when we say that throughout his
after career a boy, in nine cases out of ten, ap-
plies his Latin and Greek to no practical purposes. The remark is trite that in his shop, or
his office, in managing his estate or his family, in
playing his part as director of a bank or a railway, he is very little aided by this knowledge
he took so many years to acquire,—so little, that

generally the greater part of it drops out of his memory; and if he occasionally vents a Latin quotation or alludes to some Greek myth, it is less to throw light on the topic in hand than for the sake of effect. If we inquire what is the real motive for giving boys a classical education, we find it to be simply conformity to public opinion. Men dress their children's minds as they do their bodies, in the prevailing fashion. As the Orinoco Indian puts on his paint before leaving his hut, not with a view to any direct benefit, but because he would be ashamed to be seen without it, so a boy's drilling in Latin and Greek is insisted on, not because of their intrinsic value, but that he may not be disgraced by being found ignorant of them—that he may have "the education of a gentleman"—the badge marking a certain social position, and bringing a consequent respect.

This parallel is still more clearly displayed in the case of the other sex. In the treatment of both mind and body, the decorative element has continued to predominate in a greater degree among women than among men. Originally personal adornment occupied the attention of both sexes equally. In these latter days of civilization, however, we see that in the dress of men the regard for appearance has, in a considerable degree, yielded to the regard for comfort; while in their education the useful has of late been trenching on the ornamental. In neither direction has this change gone so far with women. The wearing of earrings, finger-rings, bracelets; the elaborate dressings of the hair; the still occasional use of paint; the immense labor bestowed in making habiliments sufficiently attractive; and the great discomfort that will be submitted to for the sake of conformity; show how greatly, in the attiring of women, the desire of approbation overrides the desire for warmth and convenience. And similarly in their education, the immense preponderance of "accomplishments" proves how here, too, use is subordinated to display. Dancing, deportment, the piano, singing, drawing—what a large space do these occupy! If you ask why Italian and German are learned, you will find that, under all the sham reasons given, the real reason is, that a knowledge of those tongues is thought ladylike. It is not that the books written in them may be utilized, which they scarcely ever are, but that Italian and German songs may be sung, and that the extent of attainment may bring whispered admiration. The births, deaths, and marriages of kings, and other like historic trivialities, are committed to memory, not because of any direct benefits that can possibly result from knowing them, but because society considers them parts of a good education—because the absence of such knowledge may bring the contempt of others. When we have named reading, writing, spelling, grammar, arithmetic, and sewing, we have named about all the things a girl is taught with a view to their direct uses in life; and even some of these have more reference to the good opinion of others than to immediate personal welfare.

Thoroughly to realize the truth that with the mind as with the body the ornamental precedes the useful, it is needful to glance at its rationale. This lies in the fact that, from the far past down even to the present, social needs have subordinated individual needs, and that the chief social need has been the control of individuals. It is not, as we commonly suppose, that there are no governments but those of monarchs, and parliaments, and constituted authorities. These acknowledged governments are supplemented by other unacknowledged ones, that grow up in all circles, in which every man or woman strives to be king or queen or lesser dignitary. To get above some and be reverenced by them, and to propitiate those who are above us, is the universal struggle in which the chief energies of life are expended. By the accumulation of wealth, by style of living, by beauty of dress, by display of knowledge or intellect, each tries to subjugate others, and so aids in weaving that ramified network of restraints by which society is kept in order. It is not the savage chief only who, in formidable war paint, with scalps at his belt, aims to strike awe into his inferiors; it is not only the belle who, by elaborate toilet, polished manners, and numerous accomplishments, strives to "make conquests"; but the scholar, the historian, the philosopher, use their acquirements to the same end. We are none of us content with quietly unfolding our own individualities to the full in all directions, but have a restless craving to impress our individualities upon others, and in some way subordinate them. And this it is which determines the character of our education. Not what knowledge is of most real worth is the consideration, but what will bring most applause, honor, respect—what will most conduce to social position and influence—what will be most imposing. As throughout life not what we are, but what we shall be thought, is the question;

so in education the question is not the intrinsic
value of knowledge so much as its extrinsic effects
on others. And this being our dominant idea,
direct utility is scarcely more regarded than by
the barbarian when filing his teeth and staining
his nails

IV

REMINISCENCES OF HIS BOYHOOD[7]

PLACES where I gathered flowers and gazed
with interest at the catkins of the hazel, have
now become places covered with ironworks, where
steam hammers make their perpetual thuds, and
through which railway-sidings everywhere ramify.
Quiet lanes in which, during early boyhood, I
went with a companion trying to catch minnows
with a hand-net in a clear little stream running
by the hedge, have been transformed into straight
roads between land-allotments, with scattered
houses built by artizans. And where I picked
blackberries, factories now stand. . . .

There was a garden of some size behind the
house containing fruit trees, and permitting a
certain amount of floriculture; and my father
rented an additional piece of land close by as
a vegetable-garden. Not infrequently I had to
join in gardening—more frequently, indeed, than

[7] From Part I, Chapter II, of the "Autobiography." Spencer's boyhood was passed in Derby. Copyright, 1904, by D.
Appleton & Co., by whose kind permission passages from
this work are printed here.

I liked. Often when I ought to have been busy at some task which my father had set to me, I was otherwise occupied—throwing stones at the birds that settled on the walls and hedges; observing the bees on the kidney-bean flowers, piercing the base of each corolla to reach the honey; or, at a disused pump-trough containing stagnant water, watching the larvæ of the gnats as they came wriggling to the surface, putting out their tails to breathe, and then descending. Most children are instinctively naturalists, and were they encouraged would readily pass from careless observations to careful and deliberate ones. My father was wise in such matters; and I was not simply allowed but encouraged to enter on natural history.

The majority of my activities, however, were those of the ordinary schoolboy, who, on Saturday afternoons and the like occasions of leisure, is commonly given to country rambles and the search for hedge-side treasures. During my early years the neighboring regions of Osmaston and Normanton were explored by me in all their details: every hedge becoming known in the course of expeditions, now in the spring seeking birds' nests, now gathering violets or dog-roses, and later in the year collecting sometimes mushrooms, sometimes blackberries, sometimes hips and haws, crab-apples and other wild products. Beyond the pleasurable exercise and the gratification to my love of adventure, there was gained during these excursions much miscellaneous knowledge of things, and the perceptions were beneficially disciplined. Of all the occupations, however, to which holidays were devoted, I delighted most in fishing. There was the river Derwent, at that time not the black dirty stream it is now, but tolerably clear and containing a fair supply of various fish; and there were the canals, which, on the whole, served better for boys' fishing. Many happy half-days, and, during the midsummer holidays, many whole days, were spent on their banks. Along with such exercise of skill as fishing itself implies, there came the exercise of skill in making fishing-tackle; for I was not so amply furnished with pocket-money that I could buy all the appliances I required. I was, I suspect, led by my father in that case, as in other cases, to use my own powers of manipulation for satisfying my needs. I made my own floats, and also "hair-tackles," as they were locally called—each some six feet of the line next the hook, made of single horse-hair instead of silk-worm gut. I remember I was cautious and systematic enough to use a test before trusting any one of them. . . .

When I was something like nine or ten years old, the love of this sport led very nearly to loss of life. I fell into deep water in the Derwent and was close upon drowning. It is a curious fact that whereas dreams are, while in progress, regarded as real, the reality was in this case taken for a dream. During the first part of my immersion I thought to myself—"Oh, it is all a dream!"; and only after coming to the surface once or twice discovered that I was actually in the water. A youth of some sixteen or seventeen plunged in and rescued me. His name was George Holme. He was at that time a mill-manager. As may be inferred from the fact that he was the one out of a considerable number of spectators who risked himself to save me, he was of superior nature morally; and he turned out in after life to be also a man of much faculty. Gradually rising, he became a wealthy manufacturer; and was led, by the development of his business, to establish trade-connections in various parts of the world—one being pushed even into Central Asia. When sixty he became mayor of Derby and magistrate. He had in a high degree that which another friend of mine describes as the business instinct—an instinct which experience tells him is quite special, and may or may not accompany other superiorities. . . .

I may here name the fact that I was in boyhood extremely prone to castle-building—a habit which continued throughout youth and into mature life: finally passing, I suppose, into the dwelling on schemes more or less practicable. In early days the habit was such that on going to bed it was a source of satisfaction to me to think I should be able to lie for a length of time and dwell on the fancies which at the time occupied me; and frequently next morning, on awaking, I was vexed with myself because I had gone to sleep before I had reveled in my imaginations as much as I had intended. Often these dreams, becoming literally day-dreams, quite filled my unconsciousness when walking. Even in the streets my state of abstraction was such that I occasionally talked aloud as I went along: a fact of which I was from time to time made aware by people who turned to look at me.

V

A TRIBUTE TO E. L. YOUMANS [8]

SOME years previously I had made the acquaintance of an American whose sympathies were enlisted on my behalf by perusal of some of my books or essays—Mr. E. A. Silsbee, of Salem, Mass. While yet the circular was in its unfinished state, I sent to him a copy, accompanied by the inquiry whether he thought that subscribers might be obtained in America. His reply, dated February 14, held out much encouragement; and a letter of March 6, written after the circular had been sent to New York, contained a sentence the significance of which was shown by subsequent events. The sentence runs—''Mr. Youmans, a very popular and intelligent lecturer on scientific subjects, well known by his works on chemistry, physiology, etc., entered with great enthusiasm into the project.'' Devoting himself with characteristic vigor to the furtherance of my scheme, this previously unknown friend succeeded in obtaining more than two hundred subscribers.

The relation thus initiated was extremely fortunate; for Prof. Edward L. Youmans [9] was of

[8] From Part VII of the "Autobiography." Copyright, 1904, by D. Appleton & Co.

[9] Spencer's debt to Professor Youmans has been well known in America. He was not only instrumental in securing the publication of his works here, but even more so in popularizing them through the *Popular Science Monthly*, of which he was the editorial founder. He had other distinction as a chemist and published a "Class Book of Chemistry" in 1852, and an "Atlas of Chemistry," in 1854.

all Americans I have known or heard of, the one most able and most willing to help me. Alike intellectually and morally, he had in the highest degrees the traits conducive to success in diffusing the doctrines he espoused; and from that time to this he has devoted his time mainly in spreading throughout the United States the doctrine of evolution. His love of wide generalizations had been shown years before in lectures on such topics as the correlation of the physical forces; and from those who heard him I have gathered that, aided by his unusual powers of exposition, the enthusiasm which contemplation of the larger truths of science produced in him was in a remarkable degree communicated to his hearers. Such larger truths, I have on many occasions observed, are those which he quickly seizes—ever passing at once through details to lay hold of essentials; and having laid hold of them, he clearly sets them forth afresh in his own way with added illustrations. But it is morally even more than intellectually that he has proved himself a true missionary of advanced ideas. Extremely energetic—so energetic that no one has been able to check his overactivity—he has expended all his powers in advancing what he holds to be the truth; and not only his powers but his means. It has proved impossible to prevent him from injuring himself in health by his exertions; and it has proved impossible to make him pay due regard to his personal interests. So that toward the close of life he finds himself wrecked in body and impoverished in estate by thirty years of devotion to high ends. Among worshipers of humanity, who teach that human welfare should be the dominant aim, I have not heard of one whose sacrifices will bear comparison with those of my friend.

VI

WHY HE NEVER MARRIED [10]

THUS, if I leave out altruistic considerations and include egoistic considerations only, I may still look back from these declining days of life with content. One drawback indeed there has been, and that a great one. All through those years in which work should have had the accompaniment of wife and children, my means were such as to render marriage impossible: I could barely support myself, much less others. And when, at length, there came adequate means the fit time had passed by. Even in this matter, however, it may be that fortune has favored me. Frequently when prospects are promising, dissatisfaction follows marriage rather than satisfaction; and in my own case the prospects would not have been promising. I am not by nature adapted to a relation in which perpetual compromise and great forbearance are needful. That extreme critical tendency which I have above described, joined with a lack of reticence no less pronounced, would, I fear, have caused perpetual domestic differences. After all, my celibate life has probably been the best for me, as well as the best for some unknown other.

[10] From Part XII of the "Autobiography." Copyright, 1904, by D. Appleton & Co.

HENRY THOMAS BUCKLE

Born in 1821, died in 1862; his father a wealthy ship-owner in London; published the first volume of his "History of Civilization" in 1857, second volume appearing in 1861; his death occurred in Syria, where he was traveling for his health; his last words "Oh, my book; I shall never finish my book."

I

THE ISOLATION OF SPAIN [1]

The Spaniards have had everything except knowledge. They have had immense wealth, and fertile and well-peopled territories in all parts of the globe. Their own country, washed by the Atlantic and Mediterranean, and possest of excellent harbors, is admirably situated for the purposes of trade between Europe and America, being so placed as to command the commerce of both hemispheres. They had, at a very early period, ample municipal privileges; they had independent parliaments; they had the right of choosing their own magistrates, and managing their own cities. They have had rich and flourishing towns, abundant manufactures, and skilful artizans, whose choice productions could secure a ready sale in every market in the world. They have cultivated the fine arts with eminent suc-

[1] From Volume II, Chapter VIII, of the "History of Civilization in England."

cess; their noble and exquisite paintings, and their magnificent churches being justly ranked among the most wonderful efforts of the human hand. They speak a beautiful, sonorous and flexible language, and their literature is not unworthy of their language. Their soil yields treasures of every kind. It overflows with wine and oil, and produces the choicest fruits in an almost tropical exuberance. It contains the most valuable minerals, in a profuse variety, unexampled in any other part of Europe. Nowhere else do we find such rare and costly marbles, so easily accessible, and in such close communication with the sea, where they might safely be shipped, and sent to countries which required them. As to the metals, there is hardly one which Spain does not possess in large quantities. Her mines of silver and quicksilver are well known. She abounds in copper, and her supply of lead is enormous. Iron and coal, the two most useful of all the productions of the inorganic world, are also abundant in that highly favored country. Iron is said to exist in every part of Spain, and to be of the best quality; while the coal mines of Asturias are described as inexhaustible. In short, nature has been so prodigal of her bounty that it has been observed with hardly an hyperbole that the Spanish nation possesses within itself nearly every natural production which can satisfy either the necessity or the curiosity of mankind.

These are splendid gifts; it is for the historian to tell how they have been used. Certainly, the people who possess them have never been deficient in natural endowments. They have had their full share of great statesmen, great kings, great magistrates, and great legislators. They have had many able and vigorous rulers; and their history is ennobled by the frequent appearance of courageous and disinterested patriots, who have sacrificed their all that they might help their country. The bravery of the people has never been disputed; while, as to the upper classes, the punctilious honor of a Spanish gentleman has passed into a byword, and circulated through the world. Of the nation generally, the best observers pronounce them to be high-minded. generous, truthful, full of integrity, warm and zealous friends, affectionate in all private relations of life, frank, charitable, and humane. Their sincerity in religious matters is unquestionable; they are, moreover, eminently temperate and frugal. Yet, all these great qualities have availed them nothing, and will avail them nothing so long as they remain ignorant. . . .

In Spain there never has been a revolution,[2] properly so called; there never has even been one grand national rebellion. The people, tho often lawless, are never free. Among them we find still preserved that peculiar taint of barbarism which makes men prefer occasional disobedience to systematic liberty. Certain feelings there are of our common nature, which even their slavish loyalty can not eradicate, and which, from time to time, urge them to resist injustice. Such instincts are happily the inalienable lot of humanity, which we can not forfeit, if we would,

---

[2] It is here to be borne in mind that Buckle wrote long before the revolutionary successes achieved by Castelar, Prim and Serrano, and the overthrow and exile of Queen Isabella in 1868.

and which are too often the last resource against
the extravagances of tyranny. And this is all
that Spain now possesses. The Spaniards, however, resist, not because they are Spaniards, but
because they are men. Still, even while they
resist, they revere. While they will rise up
against a vexatious impost, they crouch before
a system of which the impost is the smallest evil.
They smite the tax-gatherer, but fall prostrate
at the feet of the contemptible prince for whom
the tax-gatherer plies his craft; they will even
revile the troublesome and importunate monk,
or sometimes they will scoff at the sleek and
arrogant priest, while such is their infatuation
that they would risk their lives in defense of
that cruel Church which has inflicted on them
hideous calamities, but to which they still cling,
as if it were the dearest object of their affections.

Connected with these habits of mind, and in
sooth forming part of them, we find a reverence
for antiquity, and an inordinate tenacity of old
opinion, old beliefs, and old habits, which remind
us of those tropical civilizations which formerly
flourished. Such prejudices were once universal,
even in Europe; but they began to die out in
the sixteenth century, and are now, comparatively
speaking, extinct, except in Spain, where they
have always been welcomed. In that country,
they retain their original force, and produce their
natural results. By encouraging the notion that
all the truths most important to know are already
known, they repress those aspirations, and dull
that generous confidence in the future, without
which nothing really great can be achieved. A
people who regard the past with too wistful an

eye will never bestir themselves to help the onward progress. They will hardly believe that progress is possible. To them antiquity is synonymous with wisdom, and every improvement is a dangerous innovation.

In this state Europe lingered for many centuries; in this state Spain still lingers. Hence the Spaniards are remarkable for an inertness, a want of buoyancy, and an absence of hope, which, in our busy and enterprising age, isolate them from the rest of the civilized world. Believing that little can be done, they are in no hurry to do it. Believing that the knowledge they have inherited is far greater than any they can obtain, they wish to preserve their intellectual possessions whole and unimpaired; inasmuch as the least alteration in them might lessen their value. Content with what has been already bequeathed, they are excluded from that great European movement, which, first clearly perceptible in the sixteenth century, has ever since been steadily advancing, unsettling old opinion, destroying old follies, reforming and improving on every side, influencing even such barbarous countries as Russia and Turkey, but leaving Spain unscathed.

While the human intellect has been making most prodigious and unheard-of strides, while discoveries in every quarter are simultaneously pressing upon us and coming in such rapid and bewildering succession that the strongest sight, dazzled by the glare of their splendor, is unable to contemplate them as a whole; while other discoveries still more important, and still more remote from ordinary experience, are manifestly approaching, and may be seen looming in the distance whence they are now obscurely working on the advanced thinkers who are nearest to them, filling their minds with those ill-defined, restless, and almost uneasy feelings, which are the invariable harbingers of future triumph; while the veil is being rudely torn and nature, violated at all points, is forced to disclose her secrets, and reveal her structure, her economy, and her laws to the indomitable energy of man; while Europe is ringing with the noise of intellectual achievements, with which even despotic governments affect to sympathize, in order that they may divert them from their natural course, and use them as new instruments whereby to oppress yet more the liberties of the people; while, amidst this general din and excitement, the public mind, swayed to and fro, is tossed and agitated—Spain sleeps on, untroubled, unheeding, impassive, receiving no impressions from the rest of the world, and making no impressions upon it. There she lies at the further extremity of the Continent, a huge and torpid mass, the sole representative now remaining of the feelings and the knowledge of the middle ages, and, what is the worst symptom of all, she is satisfied with her own condition. Tho she is the most backward country in Europe, she believes herself to be the foremost. She is proud of everything of which she should be ashamed. She is proud of the antiquity of her opinion; proud of her orthodoxy; proud of the strength of her faith; proud of her immeasurable and childish credulity; proud of her unwillingness to amend either her creed or her customs; proud of her hatred of heretics, and proud of the undying vigilance with which she has baffled their efforts to obtain a full and legal establishment on her soil.

II

GEORGE III AND THE ELDER PITT [3]

To a superficial observer, the accession of George III was one of the most fortunate events that could have occurred. The new king was born in England, spoke English as his mother tongue, and was said to look upon Hanover as a foreign country, whose interests were to be considered of subordinate importance. At the same time, the last hopes of the House of Stuart were now destroyed; the Pretender himself was languishing in Italy, where he shortly after died: and his son, a slave to the vices which seemed hereditary in that family, was consuming his life in an unpitied and ignominious obscurity.

And yet these circumstances, which appeared so favorable, did of necessity involve the most disastrous consequences. The fear of a disputed succession being removed, the sovereign was emboldened to a course on which he otherwise would not have ventured. All those monstrous doctrines respecting the rights of kings, which the Revolution was supposed to have destroyed, were suddenly revived. The clergy, abandoning the now

[3] From Volume I, Chapter VII, of the "History of Civilization in England."

hopeless cause of the Pretender, displayed the
same zeal for the House of Hanover which they
had formerly displayed for the House of Stuart.
The pulpits resounded with praises of the new
king, of the domestic virtues, of his piety, but,
above all, his dutiful attachment to the English
Church. The result was the establishment of an
alliance between the two parties more intimate
than any had been seen in England since the
time of Charles I. Under their auspices the
old Tory faction rapidly rallied, and were soon
able to dispossess their rivals of the management
of the government.

This reactionary movement was greatly aided
by the personal character of George III, for he,
being despotic as well as superstitious, was equally anxious to extend the prerogative and
strengthen the church. Every liberal sentiment,
everything approaching to reform, nay, even the
mere mention of inquiry, was an abomination in
the eyes of that narrow and ignorant prince.
Without knowledge, without taste, without even
a glimpse of one of the sciences, or a feeling for
one of the fine arts, education had done nothing
to enlarge a mind which nature had more than
usually contracted. Totally ignorant of the history and resources of foreign countries, and
barely knowing their geographical position, his
information was scarcely more extensive respecting the people over whom he was called to rule.
In that immense mass of evidence now extant,
and which consists of every description of private
correspondence, records of private conversation
and of public acts, there is not to be found the
slightest proof that he knew any one of those

numerous things which the governor of a country ought to know; or indeed, that he was acquainted with a single duty of his position, except that mere mechanical routine of ordinary business which might have been effected by the lowest clerk in the meanest office in his kingdom.

The course of proceeding which such a king as this was likely to follow could be easily foreseen. He gathered round his throne that great party, who, clinging to the tradition of the past, have always made it their boast to check the progress of their age. During the sixty years of his reign, he, with the sole exception of Pitt, never willingly admitted to his councils a single man of great ability; not one whose name is associated with any measure of value either in domestic or in foreign policy. Even Pitt only maintained his position in the state by forgetting the lessons of his illustrious father, and abandoning those liberal principles in which he had been educated, and with which he entered public life. Because George III hated the idea of reform, Pitt not only relinquished what he had before declared to be absolutely necessary, but did not hesitate to persecute to the death the party with whom he had once associated in order to obtain it. Because George III looked upon slavery as one of those good old customs which the wisdom of his ancestors had consecrated, Pitt did not dare to use his power for procuring its abolition, but left to his successors the glory of destroying that infamous trade, on the preservation of which his royal master had set his heart. Because George III detested the French of whom he knew as much as he knew of the inhabitants of Kamchatka or of Tibet, Pitt, contrary to his own judgment, engaged in a war with France by which England was seriously imperiled, and the English people burdened with a debt that their remotest posterity will be unable to pay. But, notwithstanding all this, when Pitt, only a few years before his death, showed a determination to concede to the Irish some small share of their undoubted rights, the King dismissed him from office; and the King's friends, as they were called, exprest their indignation at the presumption of a minister who could oppose the wishes of so benign and gracious a master. And when, unhappily for his own fame, this great man determined to return to power, he could only recover office by conceding that very point for which he had relinquished it; thus setting the mischievous example of the minister of a free country sacrificing his own judgment to the personal prejudices of the sovereign.

As it was hardly possible to find other ministers who to equal abilities would add equal subservience, it is not surprizing that the highest offices were constantly filled by men of notorious incapacity. Indeed, the King seemed to have an instinctive antipathy to everything great and noble. During the reign of George II the elder Pitt had won for himself a reputation which covered the world, and had carried to an unprecedented height the glories of the English name. He, however, as the avowed friend of popular rights, strenuously opposed the despotic principles of the court; and for this reason he was hated by George III with a hatred that seemed barely compatible with a sane mind.

MATTHEW ARNOLD

Born in 1822, died in 1888; son of "Arnold of Rugby"; educated at Rugby and Oxford; fellow of Oriel; lay inspector
of schools in 1851; professor of poetry at Oxford in 1857;
visited the United States in 1883 and 1886; published "Em-
pedocles on Etna" in 1853, "Essays in Criticism" in 1865,
"Literature and Dogma" in 1873, "Culture and Anarchy"
in 1877.

THE MOTIVE FOR CULTURE [1]

THE disparagers of culture make its motive
curiosity; sometimes, indeed, they make its motive mere exclusiveness and vanity. The culture
which is supposed to plume itself on a smattering
of Greek and Latin is a culture which is begotten
by nothing so intellectual as curiosity; it is valued
either out of sheer vanity and ignorance or else
as an engine of social and class distinction, separating its holder, like a badge or title, from
other people who have not got it. No serious
man would call this culture, or attach any value
to it as culture at all. To find the real ground
for the very different estimate which serious
people will set upon culture we must find some
motive for culture in the terms of which may
lie a real ambiguity; and such a motive the word
curiosity gives us.

I have before now pointed out that we English
do not, like the foreigners, use this word in a
good sense as well as in a bad sense. With us

[1] From "Culture and Anarchy."

the word is always used in a somewhat disapproving sense. A liberal and intelligent eagerness about the things of the mind may be meant by a foreigner when he speaks of curiosity, but with us the word always conveys a certain notion of frivolous and unedifying activity. In the *Quarterly Review*, some little time ago, was an estimate of the celebrated French critic, M. Sainte-Beuve, and a very inadequate estimate of it in my judgment it was. And its inadequacy consisted chiefly in this: that in our English way it left out of sight the double sense really involved in the word curiosity, thinking enough was said to stamp M. Sainte-Beuve with blame, if it was said that he was impelled in his operations as a critic by curiosity, and omitting either to perceive that M. Sainte-Beuve himself, and many other people with him, would consider that this was praiseworthy and not blameworthy, or to point out why it ought really to be accounted worthy of blame and not of praise. For as there is a curiosity about intellectual matters which is futile, and merely a disease, so there is certainly a curiosity—a desire after the things of the mind simply for their own sakes and for the pleasure of seeing them as they are—which is, in an intelligent being, natural and laudable.

Nay, and the very desire to see things as they are implies a balance and regulation of mind which is not often attained without fruitful effort, and which is the very opposite of the blind and diseased impulse of mind which is what we mean to blame when we blame curiosity. Montesquieu says: "The first motive which ought to impel us to study is the desire to augment the excellence of our nature, and to render an intelligent being yet more intelligent.'' This is the true ground to assign for the genuine scientific passion, however manifested, and for culture, viewed simply as a fruit of this passion; and it is a worthy ground, even tho we let the term curiosity stand to describe it.

But there is of culture another view, in which not solely the scientific passion, the sheer desire to see things as they are, natural and proper in an intelligent being, appears as the ground of it. There is a view in which all the love of our neighbor, the impulses toward action, help, and beneficence, the desire for removing human error, clearing human confusion, and diminishing human misery, the noble aspiration to leave the world better and happier than we found it— motives eminently such as are called social— come in as part of the grounds of culture, and the main and preeminent part. Culture is then properly described not as having its origin in curiosity, but as having its origin in the love of perfection; it is a study of perfection. It moves by the force, not merely or primarily of the scientific passion for pure knowledge, but also of the moral and social passion for doing good. As, in the first view of it, we took for its worthy motto Montesquieu's words: ''To render an intelligent being yet more intelligent!'' so, in the second view of it, there is no better motto which it can have than these words of Bishop Wilson: ''To make reason and the will of God prevail!'' . . .

The pursuit of perfection, then, is the pursuit of sweetness and light. He who works for sweetness and light works to make reason and the will of God prevail. He who works for machinery, he who works for hatred, works only for confusion. Culture looks beyond machinery, culture hates hatred, culture has one great passion, the passion for sweetness and light. It has one even yet greater!—the passion for making them prevail. It is not satisfied till we all come to a perfect man; it knows that the sweetness and light of the few must be imperfect until the raw and unkindled masses of humanity are touched with sweetness and light. If I have not shrunk from saying that we must work for sweetness and light, so neither have I shrunk from saying that we must have a broad basis, must have sweetness and light for as many as possible. Again and again I have insisted how those are the happy moments of humanity, how those are the marking epochs of a people's life, how those are the flowering times for literature and art and all the creative power of genius, when there is a national glow of life and thought, when the whole of society is in the fullest measure permeated by thought, sensible to beauty, intelligent and alive. Only it must be real thought and real beauty; real sweetness and real light. Plenty of people will try to give the masses, as they call them, an intellectual food prepared and adapted in the way they think proper for the actual condition of the masses. The ordinary popular literature is an example of this way of working on the masses. Plenty of people will try to indoctrinate the masses with the set of ideas and judgments constituting the creed of their own profession or party.

Our religious and political organizations give an example of this way of working on the masses. I condemn neither way; but culture works differently. It does not try to teach down to the level of inferior classes; it does not try to win them for this or that sect of its own, with ready-made judgments and watchwords. It seeks to do away with classes; to make the best that has been thought and known in the world current everywhere; to make all men live in an atmosphere of sweetness and light, where they may use ideas, as it uses them itself, freely—nourished, and not bound by them. This is the social idea; and the men of culture are the true apostles of equality. The great men of culture are those who have had a passion for diffusing, for making prevail, for carrying from one end of society to the other, the best knowledge, the best ideas of their time, who have labored to divest knowledge of all that was harsh, uncouth, difficult, abstract, professional, exclusive; to humanize it; to make it efficient outside the clique of the cultivated and learned, yet still remaining the best knowledge and thought of the time, and a true source, therefore, of sweetness and light.

Such a man was Abélard in the Middle Ages, in spite of all his imperfections; and thence the boundless emotion and enthusiasm which Abélard excited. Such were Lessing and Herder in Germany, at the end of the last century; and their services to Germany were in this way inestimably precious. Generations will pass, and literary monuments will accumulate, and works far more perfect than the works of Lessing and Herder will be produced in Germany; and yet the names

of these two men will fill a German with a
reverence and enthusiasm such as the names of
the most gifted masters will hardly awaken.

And why? Because they humanized knowledge; because they broadened the basis of life
and intelligence; because they worked powerfully
to diffuse the sweetness and light, to make reason
and the will of God prevail. With Saint Augus-
tine they said: "Let us not leave thee alone
to make in the secret of thy knowledge, as thou
didst before the creation of the firmament, the
division of light from darkness; let the children
of thy spirit, placed in their firmament, make
their light shine upon the earth, mark the division of night and day, and announce the revolution of the times; for the old order is passed,
and the new arises; the night is spent, the day
is come forth; and thou shalt crown the year
with thy blessing, when thou shalt send forth
laborers into thy harvest sown by other hands
than theirs; when thou shalt send forth new
laborers to new seedtimes, whereof the harvest
shall be not yet."

EDWARD A. FREEMAN

Born in 1823, died in 1892; educated at Oxford, remaining there as a fellow until 1847, and later for many years an examiner there in Modern History; made Regius professor at Oxford in 1884; published his "Conquest of the Saracens" in 1856, "Federal Government from the Foundation of the Achaian League to the Disruption of the United States" in 1863, this work being never completed; "The Norman Conquest" in 1867-79, "Historical Essays" in 1871, "Some Impressions of the United States" in 1893 and many other volumes on general and local history.

THE DEATH OF WILLIAM THE CONQUEROR[1]

THE death-bed of William was a death-bed of all formal devotion, a death-bed of penitence which we may trust was more than formal. The English Chronicles,[2] after weighing the good and evil in him, sends him out of the world with a charitable prayer for his soul's rest; and his repentance, late and fearful as it was, at once marks the distinction between the conqueror on his bed of death and his successor cut off without a thought of penitence in the midst of his crimes. He made his will. The mammon of unrighteousness which he had gathered together amid the groans and tears of England he now strove so to dispose of as to pave his way to an everlasting habitation. All his treasures were distributed among the poor and the churches of his domin-

[1] From "The History of the Norman Conquest."
[2] William of Malmesbury.

214

ions. A special sum was set apart for the rebuilding of the churches which had been burned at Mantes, and gifts in money and books and ornaments of every kind were to be distributed among all the churches of England according to their rank. He then spoke of his own life and of the arrangements which he wished to make for his dominions after his death. The Normans, he said, were a brave and unconquered race; but they needed the curb of a strong and righteous master to keep them in the path of order. Yet the rule over them must by all law pass to Robert. Robert was his eldest born; he had promised him the Norman succession before he won the crown of England, and he had received the homage of the barons of the Duchy. Normandy and Maine must therefore pass to Robert, and for them he must be the man of the French king. Yet he well knew how sad would be the fate of the land which had to be ruled by one so proud and foolish, and for whom a career of shame and sorrow was surely doomed.

But what was to be done with England? Now at last the heart of William smote him. To England he dared not appoint a successor; he could only leave the disposal of the island realm to the Almighty Ruler of the world. The evil deeds of his past life crowded upon his soul. Now at last his heart confest that he had won England by no right, by no claim of birth; that he had won the English crown by wrong, and that what he had won by wrong he had no right to give to another. He had won his realm by warfare and bloodshed; he had treated the sons of the English soil with needless harshness; he had cruelly wronged nobles and commons; he had spoiled many men wrongfully of their inheritance; he had slain countless multitudes by hunger or by the sword. The harrying of Northumberland now rose up before his eyes in all its blackness. The dying man now told how cruelly he had burned and plundered the land, what thousands of every age and sex among the noble nation which he had conquered had been done to death at his bidding. The scepter of the realm which he had won by so many crimes he dared not hand over to any but to God alone. Yet he would not hide his wish that his son William, who had ever been dutiful to him, might reign in England after him. He would send him beyond the sea, and he would pray Lafranc to place the crown upon his head, if the Primate in his wisdom deemed that such an act could be rightly done.

Of the two sons of whom he spoke, Robert was far away, a banished rebel; William was by his bedside. By his bedside also stood his youngest son, the English Ætheling, Henry the Clerk. "And what dost thou give to me, my father?" said the youth. "Five thousand pounds of silver from my hoard," was the Conqueror's answer. "But of what use is a hoard to me if I have no place to dwell in?" "Be patient, my son, and trust in the Lord, and let thine elders go before thee." It is perhaps by the light of the later events that our chronicler goes on to make William tell his youngest son that the day would come when he would succeed both his brothers in their dominions, and would be richer and mightier than either of them. The King then dictated a letter to Lafranc, setting forth his wishes with regard to the kingdom. He sealed it and gave it to his son William, and bade him, with his last blessing and his last kiss, to cross at once into England. William Rufus straightway set forth for Witsand, and there heard of his father's death. Meanwhile Henry, too, left his father's bedside to take for himself the money that was left to him, to see that nothing was lacking in its weight, to call together his comrades on whom he could trust, and to take measures for stowing the treasure in a place of safety.

And now those who stood around the dying King began to implore his mercy for the captives whom he held in prison. He granted the prayer. . . .

The last earthly acts of the Conqueror were now done. He had striven to make his peace with God and man, and to make such provision as he could for the children and the subjects whom he had left behind him. And now his last hour was come. On a Thursday morning in September, when the sun had already risen upon the earth, the sound of the great bell of the metropolitan minster struck on the ears of the dying King. He asked why it sounded. He was told that it rang for prime in the church of our Lady. William lifted his eyes to heaven, he stretched forth his hands, and spake his last words: "To my Lady Mary, the Holy Mother of God, I commend myself, that by her holy prayers she may reconcile me to her dear Son, our Lord Jesus Christ." He prayed, and his soul passed away. William, king of the English and duke of the Normans, the man whose fame has filled

217

the world in his own and in every following age, had gone the way of all flesh. No kingdom was left him now but his seven feet of ground, and even to that his claim was not to be undisputed.

The death of a king in those days came near to a break-up of all civil society. Till a new king was chosen and crowned, there was no longer a power in the land to protect or to chastise. All bonds were loosed; all public authority was in abeyance; each man had to look to his own as he best might. No sooner was the breath out of William's body than the great company which had patiently watched around him during the night was scattered hither and thither. The great men mounted their horses and rode with all speed to their own homes, to guard their houses and goods against the outburst of lawlessness which was sure to break forth now that the land had no longer a ruler. Their servants and followers, seeing their lords gone, and deeming that there was no longer any fear of punishment, began to make spoil of the royal chamber. Weapons, clothes, vessels, the royal bed and its furniture, were carried off, and for a whole day the body of the Conqueror lay well-nigh bare on the floor of the room in which he died.

THOMAS HENRY HUXLEY

Born in 1825, died in 1895; educated at Charing Cross
Hospital, London; assistant surgeon on a naval ship in 1846-
50; professor at the Royal School of Mines and the Royal
Institute; lord rector of Aberdeen in 1874; lecturer at Cambridge in 1883; president of the Royal Society in 1883;
published, among other works, "Man's Place in Nature" in
1863, "Lay Sermons" in 1870; "Critiques and Addresses" in
1873, "Evolution and Ethics" in 1893.

ON A PIECE OF CHALK [1]

A GREAT chapter of the history of the world
is written in the chalk. Few passages in the
history of man can be supported by such an
overwhelming mass of direct and indirect evidence as that which testifies to the truth of the
fragment of the history of the globe which I
hope to enable you to read with your own eyes
to-night. Let me add that few chapters of human
history have a more profound significance for
ourselves. I weigh my words well when I assert
that the man who should know the true history
of the bit of chalk which every carpenter carries
about in his breeches pocket, tho ignorant of all
other history, is likely, if he will think his knowl-

[1] From a lecture delivered to the workingmen of Norwich,
England, during the meeting of the British Association in
1868, now included in "Lay Sermons, Addresses and Re-
views." By permission of D. Appleton & Co.

edge out to its ultimate results, to have a truer and therefore a better conception of this wonderful universe, and of man's relation to it, than the most learned student who is deep-read in the records of humanity and ignorant of those of Nature.

The language of the chalk is not hard to learn; not nearly so hard as Latin, if you only want to get at the broad features of the story it has to tell: and I propose that we now set to work to spell that story out together.

We all know that if we "burn" chalk, the result is quicklime. Chalk in fact is a compound of carbonic-acid gas and lime; and when you make it very hot, the carbonic acid flies away and the lime is left. By this method of procedure we see the lime, but we do not see the carbonic acid. If on the other hand you were to powder a little chalk and drop it into a good deal of strong vinegar, there would be a great bubbling and fizzing, and finally a clear liquid in which no sign of chalk would appear. Here you see the carbonic acid in the bubbles; the lime dissolved in the vinegar vanishes from sight. There are a great many other ways of showing that chalk is essentially nothing but carbonic acid and quicklime. Chemists enunciate the result of all the experiments which prove this, by stating that chalk is almost wholly composed of "carbonate of lime."

It is desirable for us to start from the knowledge of this fact, tho it may not seem to help us very far toward what we seek. For carbonate of lime is a widely spread substance, and is met with under very various conditions. All sorts of limestones are composed of more or less pure carbonate of lime. The crust which is often deposited by waters which have drained through limestone rocks, in the form of what are called stalagmites and stalactites, is carbonate of lime. Or to take a more familiar example, the fur on the inside of a tea-kettle is carbonate of lime; and for anything chemistry tells us to the contrary, the chalk might be a kind of gigantic fur upon the bottom of the earth-kettle, which is kept pretty hot below. . . .

But the slice of chalk presents a totally different appearance when placed under the microscope. The general mass of it is made up of very minute granules; but imbedded in this matrix are innumerable bodies, some smaller and some larger, but on a rough average not more than a hundreth of an inch in diameter, having a well-defined shape and structure. A cubic inch of some specimens of chalk may contain hundreds of thousands of these bodies, compacted together with incalculable millions of granules.

The examination of a transparent slice gives a good notion of the manner in which the components of the chalk are arranged, and of their relative proportion. But by rubbing up some chalk with a brush in water and then pouring off the milky fluid, so as to obtain sediments of different degrees of fineness, the granules and the minute rounded bodies may be pretty well separated from one another, and submitted to microscopic examination, either as opaque or as transparent objects. By combining the views obtained in these various methods, each of the rounded bodies may be proved to be a beautifully

constructed calcareous fabric, made up of a
number of chambers communicating freely with
one another. The chambered bodies are of various forms. One of the commonest is something
like a badly grown raspberry, being formed of
a number of nearly globular chambers of different
sizes congregated together. It is called Globigerina, and some specimens of chalk consist of
little else than Globigerinæ and granules. Let
us fix our attention upon the Globigerina. It is
the spore of the game we are tracking. If we
can learn what it is and what are the conditions
of its existence, we shall see our way to the origin
and past history of the chalk. . . .

The history of the discovery of these living
Globigerinæ, and of the part which they play
in rock-building, is singular enough. It is a
discovery which, like others of no less scientific
importance, has arisen incidentally out of work
devoted to very different and exceedingly practical interests. When men first took to the sea,
they speedily learned to look out for the shoals
and rocks; and the more the burden of their
ships increased, the more imperatively necessary
it became for sailors to ascertain with precision
the depth of the waters they traversed. Out of
this necessity grew the use of the lead and
sounding-line; and ultimately marine surveying,
which is the recording of the form of coasts and
of the depth of the sea, as ascertained by the
sounding-lead, upon charts.

At the same time it became desirable to ascertain and to indicate the nature of the sea
bottom, since this circumstance greatly affects
its goodness as holding-ground for anchors. Some

ingenious tar, whose name deserves a better fate than the oblivion into which it has fallen, attained this object by "arming" the bottom of the lead with a lump of grease, to which more or less of the sand or mud or broken shells, as the case might be, adhered, and was brought to the surface. But however well adapted such an apparatus might be for rough nautical purposes, scientific accuracy could not be expected from the armed lead; and to remedy its defects (especially when applied to sounding in great depths), Lieutenant Brooke of the American Navy some years ago invented a most ingenious machine, by which a considerable portion of the superficial layer of the sea bottom can be scooped out and brought up from any depth to which the lead descends. In 1853 Lieutenant Brooke obtained mud from the bottom of the North Atlantic, between Newfoundland and the Azores, at a depth of more than 10,000 feet or two miles, by the help of this sounding apparatus. The specimens were sent for examination to Ehrenberg of Berlin and to Bailey of West Point; and those able microscopists found that this deep-sea mud was almost entirely composed of the skeletons of living organisms—the greater proportion of these being just like the Globigerinæ already known to occur in the chalk.

Thus far the work had been carried on simply in the interests of science; but Lieutenant Brooke's method of sounding acquired a high commercial value when the enterprise of laying down the telegraph cable between this country and the United States was undertaken. For it became a matter of immense importance to know not only the depth of the sea over the whole line along which the cable was to be laid, but the exact nature of the bottom, so as to guard against chances of cutting or fraying the strands of that costly rope. The Admiralty consequently ordered Captain Dayman, an old friend and shipmate of mine, to ascertain the depth over the whole line of the cable and to bring back specimens of the bottom. In former days, such a command as this might have sounded very much like one of the impossible things which the young prince in the fairy tales is ordered to do before he can obtain the hand of the princess. However, in the months of June and July, 1857, my friend performed the task assigned to him with great expedition and precision, without, so far as I know, having met with any reward of that kind. The specimens of Atlantic mud which he procured were sent to me to be examined and reported upon.

The results of all these operations is, that we know the contours and the nature of the surface soil covered by the North Atlantic for a distance of 1,700 miles from east to west, as well as we know that of any part of the dry land. It is a prodigious plain—one of the widest and most even plains in the world. If the sea were drained off, you might drive a wagon all the way from Valentia on the west coast of Ireland, to Trinity Bay in Newfoundland; and except upon one sharp incline about 200 miles from Valentia, I am not quite sure that it would even be necessary to put the skid on, so gentle are the ascents and descents upon that long route. From Valentia the road would lie downhill for about 200 miles, to the point at which the bottom is now covered by 1,700 fathoms of sea-water. Then would come the central plain, more than a thousand miles wide, the inequalities of the surface of which would be hardly perceptible, tho the depth of water upon it now varies from 10,000 to 15,000 feet; and there are places in which Mont Blanc might be sunk without showing its peak above water. Beyond this the ascent on the American side commences, and gradually leads for about 300 miles to the Newfoundland shore.

Almost the whole of the bottom of this central plain (which extends for many hundred miles in a north-and-south direction) is covered by a fine mud, which when brought to the surface dries into a grayish-white friable substance. You can write with this on a blackboard if you are so inclined; and to the eye it is quite like very soft, grayish chalk. Examined chemically, it proves to be composed almost wholly of carbonate of lime; and if you make a section of it, in the same way as that of the piece of chalk was made, and view it with the microscope, it presents innumerable Globigerinæ imbedded in a granular matrix. Thus this deep-sea mud is substantially chalk. I say substantially, because there are a good many minor differences; but as these have no bearing on the question immediately before us—which is the nature of the Globigerinæ of the chalk—it is unnecessary to speak of them.

Globigerinæ of every size, from the smallest to the largest, are associated together in the Atlantic mud, and the chambers of many are filled by a soft animal matter. This soft substance is, in fact, the remains of the creature to which the Globigerina shell, or rather skeleton, owes its existence, and which is an animal of the simplest imaginable description. It is, in fact, a mere particle of living jelly, without defined parts of any kind; without a mouth, nerves, muscles, or distinct organs, and only manifesting its vitality to ordinary observation by thrusting out and retracting from all parts of its surface long filamentous processes, which serve for arms and legs. Yet this amorphous particle, devoid of everything which in the higher animals we call organs, is capable of feeding, growing, and multiplying; of separating from the ocean the small proportion of carbonate of lime which is dissolved in sea-water; and of building up that substance into a skeleton for itself, according to a pattern which can be imitated by no other known agency.

The notion that animals can live and flourish in the sea, at the vast depths from which apparently living Globigerinæ have been brought up, does not agree very well with our usual conceptions respecting the conditions of animal life; and it is not so absolutely impossible as it might at first sight appear to be, that the Globigerinæ of the Atlantic sea bottom do not live and die where they are found.

As I have mentioned, the soundings from the great Atlantic plain are almost entirely made up of Globigerinæ, with the granules which have been mentioned, and some few other calcareous shells; but a small percentage of the chalky mud —perhaps at most some five per cent. of it—is of a different nature, and consists of shells and skeletons composed of silex or pure flint. These siliceous bodies belong partly to the lowly vegetable organisms which are called Diatomaceæ, and partly to the minute and extremely simple animals termed Radiolaria. It is quite certain that these creatures do not live at the bottom of the ocean, but at its surface, where they may be obtained in prodigious numbers by the use of a properly constructed net. Hence it follows that these siliceous organisms, tho they are not heavier than the lightest dust, must have fallen in some cases through 15,000 feet of water before they reached their final resting-place on the ocean floor. And considering how large a surface these bodies expose in proportion to their weight, it is probable that they occupy a great length of time in making their burial journey from the surface of the Atlantic to the bottom. . . .

Thus not only is it certain that the chalk is the mud of an ancient sea bottom, but it is no less certain that the chalk sea existed during an extremely long period, tho we may not be prepared to give a precise estimate of the length of that period in years. The relative duration is clear, tho the absolute duration may not be definable. The attempt to affix any precise date to the period at which the chalk sea began or ended its existence is baffled by difficulties of the same kind. But the relative age of the cretaceous epoch may be determined with as great ease and certainty as the long duration of that epoch.

You will have heard of the interesting discoveries recently made in various parts of western Europe, of flint implements, obviously worked into shape by human hands, under circumstances which show conclusively that man is a very ancient denizen of these regions. It has been proved that the whole population of Europe whose existence has been revealed to us in this way, consisted of savages such as the Eskimo are now; that in the country which is now France they hunted the reindeer, and were familiar with the ways of the mammoth and the bison. The physical geography of France was in those days different from what it is now,—the river Somme, for instance, having cut its bed a hundred feet deeper between that time and this; and it is probable that the climate was more like that of Canada or Siberia than that of western Europe.

The existence of these people is forgotten even in the traditions of the oldest historical nations. The name and fame of them had utterly vanished until a few years back; and the amount of physical change which has been effected since their day renders it more than probable that, venerable as are some of the historical nations, the workers of the chipped flints of Hoxne or of Amiens are to them as they are to us in point of antiquity. But if we assign to these hoar relics of long-vanished generations of men the greatest age that can possibly be claimed for them, they are not older than the drift of boulder clay, which in comparison with the chalk is but a very juvenile deposit. You need go no further than your own seaboard for evidence of this fact. At one of the most charming spots on the coast of Norfolk, Cromer, you will see the boulder clay forming a vast mass, which lies upon the chalk, and must consequently have come into existence after it. Huge boulders of chalk are in fact included in the clay, and have evidently been brought to the position they now occupy by the same agency as that which has planted blocks of syenite from Norway side by side with them. . . .

Thus there is a writing upon the wall of cliffs at Cromer, and whoso runs may read it. It tells us with an authority which can not be impeached, that the ancient sea-bed of the chalk sea was raised up and remained dry land until it was covered with forest, stocked with the great game the spoils of which have rejoiced your geologists. How long it remained in that condition can not be said; but "the whirligig of time brought its revenges" in those days as in these. That dry land with the bones and teeth of generations of long-lived elephants, hidden away among the gnarled roots and dry leaves of its ancient trees, sank gradually to the bottom of the icy sea, which covered it with huge masses of drift and boulder clay. Sea beasts such as the walrus, now restricted to the extreme north, paddled about where birds had twittered among the topmost twigs of the fir-trees. How long this state of things endured we know not, but at length it came to an end. The upheaved glacial mud hardened into the soil of modern Norfolk. Forests grew once more, the wolf and the beaver replaced the reindeer and the elephant; and at length what we call the history of England dawned.

FREDERIC HARRISON

Born in 1831; educated at Oxford; one of the founders of
the Positivist School; Professor of Jurisprudence and Inter-
national Law at Lincoln's Inn Hall, 1877-89; alderman of
London in 1889-92; published "The Meaning of History" in
1862; "The Choice of Books" in 1886; "Oliver Cromwell"
in 1889; "Victorian Literature" in 1895; a Life of Ruskin
in 1902; a book on Washington in 1902.

THE GREAT BOOKS OF THE WORLD [1]

I SAY it most confidently, the first intellectual
task of our age is rightly to order and make
serviceable the vast realm of printed material
which four centuries have swept across our path.
To organize our knowledge, to systematize our
reading, to save, out of the relentless cataract of
ink, the immortal thoughts of the greatest—this
is a necessity unless the productive ingenuity of
man is to lead us at last to a measureless and
pathless chaos. To know anything that turns up
is, in the infinity of knowledge, to know nothing.
To read the first book we come across, in the
wilderness of books, is to learn nothing. To turn
over the pages of ten thousand volumes is to be
practically indifferent to all that is good. . . .

[1] From an address on "The Choice of Books," read before
the London Institution in the winter of 1878-79, and afterward made the basis of Mr. Harrison's book having the
same title.

I am very far from meaning that our whole
time spent with books is to be given to study.
Far from it. I put the poetic and emotional side
of literature as the most needed for daily use. I
take the books that seek to rouse the imagination,
to stir up feeling, touch the heart; the books of
art, of fancy, of ideals, such as reflect the delight
and aroma of life. And here how does the trivial,
provided it is the new, that which stares at us in
the advertising columns of the day, crowd out the
immortal poetry and pathos of the human race,
vitiating our taste for those exquisite pieces which
are a household word, and weakening our mental
relish for the eternal works of genius! Old Homer
is the very fountainhead of pure poetic enjoyment, of all that is spontaneous, simple, native,
and dignified in life. He takes us into the am-
brosial world of heroes, of human vigor, of purity,
of grace. Now Homer is one of the few poets
the life of whom can be fairly preserved in a
translation. Most men and women can say that
they have read Homer, just as most of us can
say that we have studied Johnson's Dictionary.
But how few of us take him up, time after time,
with fresh delight! How few have even read the
entire "Iliad" and "Odyssey" through! Whether
in the resounding lines of the old Greek, as fresh
and ever-stirring as the waves that tumble on the
seashore, filling the soul with satisfying silent
wonder at its restless unison; whether in the
quaint lines of Chapman, or the clarion couplets
of Pope, or the closer versions of Cowper, Lord
Derby, of Philip Worsley, or even in the new
prose version of the "Odyssey," Homer is always
fresh and rich. And yet how seldom does one

find a friend spellbound over the Greek Bible of antiquity, whilst they wade through torrents of magazine quotations from a petty versifier of to-day, and in an idle vacation will graze, as contentedly as cattle in a fresh meadow, through the chopped straw of a circulating library. A generation which will listen to "Pinafore" for three hundred nights, and will read M. Zola's seventeenth romance, can no more read Homer than it could read a cuneiform inscription. It will read about Homer just as it will read about a cuneiform inscription, and will crowd to see a few pots which probably came from the neighborhood of Troy. But to Homer and the primeval type of heroic man in his beauty, and his simpleness, and joyousness, the cultured generation is really dead, as completely as some spoiled beauty of the ball-room is dead to the bloom of the heather or the waving of the daffodils in a glade.

It is a true psychological problem, this nausea which idle culture seems to produce for all that is manly and pure in heroic poetry. One knows—at least every schoolboy has known—that a passage of Homer, rolling along in the hexameter or trumped out by Pope, will give one a hot glow of pleasure and raise a finer throb in the pulse; one knows that Homer is the easiest, most artless, most diverting of all poets; that the fiftieth reading rouses the spirit even more than the first—and yet we find ourselves (we are all alike) painfully pshaw-ing over some new and uncut barley sugar in rime, which a man in the street asked us if we had read, or it may be some learned lucubration about the site of Troy by some one we chanced to meet at dinner. It is an unwritten chapter in the history of the human mind, how this literary prurience after new print unmans us for the enjoyment of the old songs chanted forth in the sunrise of human imagination. To ask a man or woman who spends half a lifetime in sucking magazines and new poems to read a book of Homer would be like asking a butcher's boy to whistle "Adelaida." The noises and sights and talk, the whirl and volatility of life around us, are too strong for us. A society which is forever gossiping in a sort of perpetual "drum" loses the very faculty of caring for anything but "early copies" and the last tale out. Thus, like the tares in the noble parable of the Sower, a perpetual chatter about books chokes the seed which is sown in the greatest books in the world.

I speak of Homer, but fifty other great poets and creators of eternal beauty would serve my argument as well. Take the latest perhaps in the series of the world-wide and immortal poets of the whole human race—Walter Scott. We all read Scott's romances, as we have all read Hume's "History of England," but how often do we read them, how zealously, with what sympathy and understanding? I am told that the last discovery of modern culture is that Scott's prose is commonplace; that the young men at our universities are far too critical to care for his artless sentences and flowing descriptions. They prefer Mr. Swinburne, Mr. Mallock, and the euphuism of young Oxford, just as some people prefer a Dresden shepherdess to the Caryatides of the Erechtheum, pronounce Fielding to be low, and Mozart to be *passé*. As boys love lollipops, so these juvenile fops love to roll phrases about under the tongue, as if phrases in themselves had a value apart from thoughts, feelings, great conceptions, or human sympathy.

For Scott is just one of the poets (we may call poets all the great creators in prose or in verse) of whom one never wearies, just as one can listen to Beethoven or watch the sunrise or the sunset day by day with new delight. I think I can read the "Antiquary," or the "Bride of Lammermoor," "Ivanhoe," "Quentin Durward," and "Old Mortality," at least once a year afresh. Now Scott is a perfect library in himself. A constant reader of romances would find that it needed months to go through even the best pieces of the inexhaustible painter of eight full centuries and every type of man, and he might repeat the process of reading him ten times in a lifetime without a sense of fatigue or sameness.

The poetic beauty of Scott's creations is almost the least of his great qualities. It is the universality of his sympathy that is so truly great, the justice of his estimates, the insight into the spirit of each age, his intense absorption of self in the vast epic of human civilization. What are the old almanacs that they so often give us as histories beside these living pictures of the ordered succession of ages? As in Homer himself, we see in this prose "Iliad" of modern history the battle of the old a d the new, the heroic defense of ancient strongholds, the long impending and inevitable doom of medieval life. Strong men and proud women struggle against the destiny of modern society, unconsciously working out its ways, undauntedly defying its power. How just is our island Homer! Neither Greek nor

Trojan sways him; Achilles is his hero; Hector is his favorite; he loves the councils of chiefs and the palace of Priam; but the swineherd, the charioteer, the slave girl, the hound, the beggar, and the herdsman, all glow alike in the harmonious coloring of his peopled epic. We see the dawn of our English nation, the defense of Christendom against the Koran, the grace and the terror of feudalism, the rise of monarchy out of baronies, the rise of parliaments out of monarchy, the rise of industry out of serfage, the pathetic ruin of chivalry, the splendid death struggle of Catholicism, the sylvan tribes of the mountain (remnants of our prehistoric forefathers) beating themselves to pieces against the hard advance of modern industry; we see the grim heroism of the Bible martyrs, the catastrophe of feudalism overwhelmed by a practical age which knew little of its graces and almost nothing of its virtues.

Such is Scott, who, we may say, has done for the various phases of modern history what Shakespeare has done for the manifold types of human character. And this glorious and most human and most historical of poets, without whom our very conception of human development would have ever been imperfect, this manliest and truest and widest of romancers we neglect for some hot-house hybrid of psychological analysis, for the wretched imitators of Balzac and the jackanapes phrasemongering of some Osric of the day, who assures us that Scott is an absolute Philistine.

In speaking with enthusiasm of Scott, as of Homer, or of Shakespeare, or of Milton, or of any of the accepted masters of the world, I have no wish to insist dogmatically upon any single name, or two or three in particular. Our enjoyment and reverence of the great poets of the world is seriously injured nowadays by the habit we get of singling out some particular quality, some particular school of art for intemperate praise or, still worse, for intemperate abuse. Mr. Ruskin, I suppose, is answerable for the taste for this one-sided and spasmodic criticism; and every young gentleman who has the trick of a few adjectives will languidly vow that Marlowe is supreme, or Murillo foul. It is the mark of rational criticism as well as of healthy thought to maintain an evenness of mind in judging of great works, to recognize great qualities in due proportion, to feel that defects are made up by beauties, and beauties are often balanced by weakness. The true judgment implies a weighing of each work and each workman as a whole, in relation to the sum of human cultivation and the gradual advance of the movement of ages. And in this matter we shall usually find that the world is right, the world of the modern centuries and the nations of Europe together. It is unlikely, to say the least of it, that a young person who has hardly ceased making Latin verses will be able to reverse the decisions of the civilized world; and it is even more unlikely that Milton and Molière, Fielding and Scott, will ever be displaced by a poet who has unaccountably lain hid for one or two centuries.

I know that in the style of to-day I ought hardly to venture to address you about poetry unless I am prepared to unfold to you the mysterious beauties of some unknown genius who has recently been unearthed by the Children of Light

and Sweetness. I confess I have no such discovery to announce. I prefer to dwell in Gath
and to pitch my tents in Ashdod; and I doubt
the use of the sling as a weapon in modern war.
I decline to go into hyperbolic eccentricities over
unknown geniuses, and a single quality or power
is not enough to arouse my enthusiasm. It is possible that no master ever painted a buttercup
like this one, or the fringe of a robe like that
one; that this poet has a unique subtlety, and that
an undefinable music. I am still unconvinced, tho
the man who can not see it, we are told, should
at once retire to the place where there is wailing
and gnashing of teeth.

I am against all gnashing of teeth, whether for
or against a particular idol. I stand by the men,
and by all the men, who have moved mankind to
the depths of their souls, who have taught generations, and formed our life. If I say of Scott, that
to have drunk in the whole of his glorious spirit
is a liberal education in itself, I am asking for no
exclusive devotion to Scott, to any poet, or any
school of poets, or any age, or any country, to
any style or any order of poet, one more than another. They are as various, fortunately, and as
many-sided as human nature itself. If I delight
in Scott, I love Fielding, and Richardson, and
Sterne, and Goldsmith, and Defoe. Yes, and I
will add Cooper and Marryat, Miss Edgeworth
and Miss Austen—to confine myself to those who
are already classics, to our own country, and to
one form of art alone, and not to venture on the
ground of contemporary romance in general.

What I have said of Homer, I would say in a
degree, but somewhat lower, of those great An-

cients who are the most accessible to us in English — Æschylus, Aristophanes, Virgil, and Horace. What I have said of Shakespeare I would say of Calderon, of Molière, of Corneille, of Racine, of Voltaire, of Alfieri, of Goethe, of those dramatists, in many forms, and with genius the most diverse, who have so steadily set themselves to idealize the great types of public life and of the phases of human history. Let us all beware lest worship of the idiosyncrasy of our peerless Shakespeare blind us to the value of the great masters who in a different world and with different aims have presented the development of civilization in a series of dramas, where the unity of a few great types of man and of society is made paramount to subtlety of character or brilliancy of language.

What I have said of Milton, I would say of Dante, or Ariosto, of Petrarch, and of Tasso; nor less would I say it of Boccaccio and Chaucer, of Camoens and Spenser, of Rabelais and of Cervantes, of Gil Blas and the Vicar of Wakefield, of Byron and of Shelley, of Goethe and of Schiller. Nor let us forget those wonderful idealizations of awakening thought and primitive societies, the pictures of other races and types of life removed from our own: all those primeval legends, ballads, songs, and tales, those proverbs, apologs, and maxims, which have come down to us from distant ages of man's history—the old idyls and myths of the Hebrew race; the tales of Greece, of the Middle Ages of the East; the fables of the Old and the New World; the songs of the Nibelungs; the romances of early feudalism; the "Morte d'Arthur"; the "Arabian

Nights''; the ballads of the early nations of Europe.

I protest that I am devoted to no school in particular: I condemn no school; I reject none. I am for the school of all the great men; and I am against the school of the smaller men. I care for Wordsworth as well as for Byron, for Burns as well as Shelley, for Boccaccio as well as for Milton, for Bunyan as well as Rabelais, for Cervantes as much as for Dante, for Corneille as well as for Shakespeare, for Goldsmith as well as Goethe. I stand by the sentence of the world; and I hold that in a matter so human and so broad as the highest poetry the judgment of the nations of Europe is pretty well settled, at any rate, after a century or two of continuous reading and discussing. Let those who will assure us that no one can pretend to culture unless he swear by Fra Angelico and Sandro Botticelli, by Arnolpho the son of Lapo, or the Lombardic bricklayers, by Martini and Galuppi (all, by the way, admirable men of the second rank); and so, in literature and poetry, there are some who will hear of nothing but Webster or Marlowe; Blake, Herrick or Keats; William Langland or the Earl of Surrey; Heine or Omar Khayyám. All of these are men of genius, and each with a special and inimitable gift of his own. But the busy world, which does not hunt poets as collectors hunt for curios, may fairly reserve these lesser lights for the time when they know the greatest well.

So, I say, think mainly of the greatest, of the best known, of those who cover the largest area of human history and man's common nature. Now when we come to count up these names accepted by the unanimous voice of Europe, we have some thirty or forty names, and amongst them are some of the most voluminous of writers. I have been running over but one department of literature alone, the poetic. I have been naming those only, whose names are household words with us, and the poets for the most part of modern Europe. Yet even here we have a list which is usually found in not less than a hundred volumes at least.

Now poetry and the highest kind of romance are exactly that order of literature, which not only will bear to be read many times, but that of which the true value can only be gained by frequent, and indeed habitual reading. A man can hardly be said to know the twelfth Mass or the ninth Symphony, by virtue of having once heard them played ten years ago; he can hardly be said to take air and exercise because he took a country walk once last autumn. And so he can hardly be said to know Scott, or Shakespeare, Molière, or Cervantes, when he once read them since the close of his school-days, or amidst the daily grind of his professional life. The immortal and universal poets of our race are to be read and reread till their music and their spirit are a part of our nature; they are to be thought over and digested till we live in the world they created for us; they are to be read devoutly, as devout men read their Bibles and fortify their hearts with psalms. For as the old Hebrew singer heard the heavens declare the glory of their Maker, and the firmament showing his handiwork, so in the long roll of poetry we see transfigured the strength and beauty of humanity, the dignity and struggles, the long life-history of our common kind. . . .

In an age of steam it seems almost idle to speak of Dante, the most profound, the most meditative, the most prophetic of all poets, in whose epic the panorama of medieval life, of feudalism at its best and Christianity at its best, stands, as in a microcosm, transfigured, judged, and measured. To most men, the ''Paradise Lost,'' with all its mighty music and its idyllic pictures of human nature, of our first-child parents in their naked purity and their awakening thought, is a serious and ungrateful task—not to be ranked with the simple enjoyments; it is a possession to be acquired only by habit. The great religious poets, the imaginative teachers of the heart, are never easy reading. But the reading of them is a religious habit, rather than an intellectual effort. I pretend not now to be dealing with a matter so deep and high as religion, or indeed with education in the fuller sense. I will say nothing of that side of reading which is really hard study, an effort of duty, matter of meditation and reverential thought.

JOHN RICHARD GREEN

Born in Oxford in 1837, died in 1883; graduated from
Oxford in 1850; a curate in London in 1860; incumbent of
St. Philip's, Stepney, in 1866; librarian at Lambeth in
1869; published his "Short History of the English People"
in 1874, "A History of the English People" in 1877-80,
"The Making of England" in 1882.

GEORGE WASHINGTON [1]

CHATHAM'S measure was contemptuously re-
jected by the lords, as was a similar measure of
Burke's by the house of commons, and a petition
of the city of London in favor of the colonies by
the king himself. With the rejection of these
efforts for conciliation began the great struggle
which ended eight years later in the severance of
the American colonies from the British crown.
The congress of delegates from the colonial legis-
latures at once voted measures for general defense, ordered the levy of an army, and set George
Washington at its head. No nobler figure ever
stood in the forefront of a nation's life. Washington was grave and courteous in address; his
manners were simple and unpretending; his
silence and the serene calmness of his temper
spoke of a perfect self-mastery. But there was
little in his outer bearing to reveal the grandeur
of soul which lifts his figure, with all the simple
majesty of an ancient statue, out of the smaller

[1] From Book IV, Chapter II of the "History of the English
People."

242

passions, the meaner impulses of the world around him. What recommended him for command was simply his weight among his fellow-land-owners of Virginia, and the experience of war which he had gained by service in border contests with the French and the Indians, as well as in Braddock's luckless expedition against Fort Duquesne.

It was only as the weary fight went on that the colonists discovered, however slowly and imperfectly, the greatness of their leader; his clear judgment, his heroic endurance, his silence under difficulties, his calmness in the hour of danger or defeat; the patience with which he waited, the quickness and hardness with which he struck, the lofty and serene sense of duty that never swerved from its task through resentment or jealousy; that never, through war or peace, felt the touch of a meaner ambition; that knew no aim save that of guarding the freedom of his fellow-countrymen, and no personal longing save that of returning to his own fireside when their freedom was secured. It was almost unconsciously that men learned to cling to Washington with a trust and faith such as few other men have won, and to regard him with a reverence which still hushes us in presence of his memory. But even America hardly recognized his real greatness while he lived. It was only when death set its seal on him that the voice of those whom he had served so long proclaimed him "the man first in war, first in peace, and first in the hearts of his fellow-countrymen."

JOHN MORLEY

Born in 1838; graduated from Oxford in 1859; editor of the *Fortnightly Review* in 1867, and of *The Pall Mall Gazette* in 1880; elected to Parliament in 1883; made Chief Secretary for Ireland in 1886, and again in 1892; made Secretary for India in 1906; published "Edmund Burke" in 1867; "Voltaire" in 1872; "Rousseau" in 1876; a "Life of Richard Cobden" in 1881; and a "Life of Gladstone" in 1904.

VOLTAIRE AS AN AUTHOR AND AS A MAN OF ACTION [1]

THE man of letters, usually unable to conceive loftier services to mankind or more attractive aims to persons of capacity than the composition of books, has treated these pretensions of Voltaire with a supercilious kind of censure, which teaches us nothing about Voltaire, while it implies a particularly shallow idea alike of the position of the mere literary life in the scale of things, and of the conditions under which the best literary work is done. To have really contributed in the humblest degree, for instance, to a peace between Prussia and her enemies in 1759, would have been an immeasurably greater performance for mankind than any given book which Voltaire could have written. And, what is still better worth observing, Voltaire's books would not have been the powers they were, but for this constant desire of his to come into the closest contact with the practical affairs of the world. He who has never left the life of a recluse, drawing an in-

[1] From "Voltaire."

244

come from the funds and living in a remote garden, constructing past, present, and future, out of his own consciousness, is not qualified either to lead mankind safely, or to think on the course of human affairs correctly. Every page of Voltaire has the bracing air of the life of the world in it, and the instinct which led him to seek the society of the conspicuous actors on the great scene was essentiall; a right one.

The book-writer takes good advantage of his opportunity to assure men expressly or by implication that he is their true king, and that the sacred bard is a mightier man than his hero. Voltaire knew better. Tho himself perhaps the most puissant man of letters that ever lived, he rated literature as it ought to be rated below action, not because written speech is less of a force, but because the speculation and criticism of the literature that substantially influences the world, make far less demand than the actual conduct of great affairs on qualities which are not rare in detail, but are amazingly rare in combination,— on temper, foresight, solidity, daring,—on strength, in a word, strength of intelligence and strength of character. Gibbon rightly amended his phrase, when he described Boethius not as stooping, but rather as rising, from his life of placid meditation to an active share in the imperial business. That he held this sound opinion is quite as plausible an explanation of Voltaire's anxiety to know persons of station and importance, as the current theory that he was of sycophantic nature. ''Why,'' he asks, ''are the ancient historians so full of light? It is because the writer had to do with public business; it is because he could be magistrate, priest, soldier; and because if he could not rise to the highest functions of the state, he had at least to make himself worthy of them. I admit," he concludes, "that we must not expect such an advantage with us, for our own constitution happens to be against it;" but he was deeply sensible what an advantage it was that they thus lost.

In short, on all sides, whatever men do and think was real and alive to Voltaire. Whatever had the quality of interesting any imaginable temperament, had the quality of interesting him. There was no subject which any set of men have ever cared about, which, if he once had mention of it, Voltaire did not care about likewise. And it was just because he was so thoroughly alive himself, that he filled the whole era with life. The more closely one studies the various movements of that time, the more clear it becomes that, if he was not the original center and first fountain of them all, at any rate he made many channels ready and gave the sign. He was the initial principle of fermentation throughout that vast commotion. We may deplore, if we think fit, as Erasmus deplored in the case of Luther, that the great change was not allowed to work itself out slowly, calmly, and without violence and disruption. These graceful regrets are powerless, and on the whole they are very enervating. Let us make our account with the actual, rather than seek excuses for self-indulgence in pensive preference of something that might have been. Practically in these great circles of affairs, what only might have been is as tho it could not be; and to know this may well suffice for us.

ROBERT LOUIS STEVENSON

Born in 1850, died in 1894; poet and essayist; his father a
noted lighthouse engineer; educated at Edinburgh University;
lived in Samoa after 1889; among his first books were "An
Inland Voyage" published in 1878; "Travels with a Donkey"
in 1879; "Virginibus Puerisque" in 1881; his works collected after his death.

I

FRANCIS VILLON'S TERRORS[1]

No sooner had the theft been accomplished than
Villon shook himself, jumped to his feet, and began helping to scatter and extinguish the embers.
Meanwhile Montigny opened the door and cau-
tiously peered into the street. The coast was
clear; there was no meddlesome patrol in sight.
Still it was judged wiser to slip out severally;
and as Villon was himself in a hurry to escape
from the neighborhood of the dead Thevenin, and
the rest were in a still greater hurry to get rid
of him before he should discover the loss of his
money, he was the first by general consent to
issue forth into the street.

The wind had triumphed and swept all the
clouds from heaven. Only a few vapors, as thin
as moonlight, fleeted rapidly across the stars.
It was bitter cold; and by a common optical effect,

[1] From "A Lodging for the Night: A Story of Francis
Villon," in the volume entitled "New Arabian Nights," published in 1882.

247

things seemed almost more definite than in the broadest daylight. The sleeping city was absolutely still; a company of white hoods, a field full of little Alps, below the twinkling stars. Villon cursed his fortune. Would it were still snowing! Now, wherever he went, he left an indelible trail behind him on the glittering streets; wherever he went he was still tethered to the house by the cemetery of St. John; wherever he went he must weave, with his own plodding feet, the rope that bound him to the crime and would bind him to the gallows. The leer of the dead man came back to him with a new significance. He snapt his fingers as if to pluck up his own spirits, and choosing a street at random, stept boldly forward in snow.

Two things preoccupied him as he went: the aspect of the gallows at Montfaucon in this bright, windy phase of the night's existence, for one; and for another, the look of the dead man with his bald head and garland of red curls. Both struck cold upon his heart, and he kept quickening his pace as if he could escape from unpleasant thoughts by mere fleetness of foot. Sometimes he looked back over his shoulder with a sudden nervous jerk; but he was the only moving thing in the white streets, except when the wind swooped around a corner and threw up the snow, which was beginning to freeze, in spouts of glittering dust.

Suddenly he saw, a long way before him, a black clump and a couple of lanterns. The clump was in motion, and the lanterns swung as tho carried by men walking. It was a patrol. And tho it was merely crossing his line of march he

judged it wiser to get out of eyeshot as speedily
as he could. He was not in the humor to be
challenged, and he was conscious of making a
very conspicuous mark upon the snow. Just on
his left hand there stood a great hotel, with some
turrets and a large porch before the door; it was
half-ruinous, he remembered, and had long stood
empty; and so he made three steps of it, and
jumped into the shelter of the porch. It was
pretty dark inside, after the glimmer of the snowy
streets, and he was groping forward with out-
spread hands, when he stumbled over some substance which offered an indescribable mixture of
resistances, hard and soft, firm and loose. His
heart gave a leap, and he sprang two steps back
and stared dreadfully at the obstacle. Then he
gave a little laugh of relief. It was only a woman,
and she dead. He knelt beside her to make sure
upon this latter point. She was freezing cold, and
rigid like a stick. A little ragged finery fluttered
in the wind about her hair, and her cheeks had
been heavily rouged that same afternoon. Her
pockets were quite empty; but in her stocking,
underneath the garter, Villon found two of the
small coins that went by the name of whites. It
was little enough; but it was always something;
and the poet was moved with a deep sense of
pathos that she should have died before she had
spent her money. That seemed to him a dark
and pitiable mystery; and he looked from the
coins in his hand to the dead woman, and back
again to the coins, shaking his head over the
riddle of man's life. Henry V of England, dying
at Vincennes just after he had conquered France,
and this poor jade cut off by a cold draft in a

great man's doorway, before she had time to spend her couple of whites—it seemed a cruel way to carry on the world. Two whites would have taken such a little while to squander; and yet it would have been one more good taste in the mouth, one more smack of the lips, before the devil got the soul, and the body was left to birds and vermin. He would like to use all his tallow before the light was blown out and the lantern broken.

While these thoughts were passing through his mind, he was feeling, half mechanically, for his purse. Suddenly his heart stopt beating; a feeling of cold scales passed up the back of his legs, and a cold blow seemed to fall upon his scalp. He stood petrified for a moment; then he felt again with one feverish movement; and then his loss burst upon him, and he was covered at once with perspiration. To spendthrifts money is so living and actual—it is such a thin veil between them and their pleasures! There is only one limit to their fortune—that of time; and a spendthrift with only a few crowns is the Emperor of Rome until they are spent. For such a person to lose his money is to suffer the most shocking reverse, and fall from heaven to hell, from all to nothing, in a breath. And all the more if he has put his head in the halter for it; if he may be hanged to-morrow for that same purse, so dearly earned, so foolishly departed! Villon stood and curst; he threw the two whites into the street; he shook his fist at heaven; he stamped, and was not horrified to find himself trampling the poor corpse. Then he began rapidly to retrace his steps toward the house beside the cemetery. He had forgotten

all fear of the patrol, which was long gone by at
any rate, and had no idea but that of his lost
purse. It was in vain that he looked right and
left upon the snow: nothing was to be seen. He
had not dropt it in the streets. Had it fallen in
the house? He would have liked dearly to go in
and see; but the idea of the grizzly occupant un-
manned him. And he saw besides, as he drew
near, that their efforts to put out the fire had been
unsuccessful; on the contrary, it had broken into
a blaze, and a changeful light played in the chinks
of door and window, and revived his terror for
the authorities and Paris gibbet.

II

THE LANTERN BEARERS [2]

THESE boys congregated every autumn about a
certain easterly fisher-village, where they tasted
in a high degree the glory of existence. The place
was created seemingly on purpose for the diver-
sion of young gentlemen. A street or two of
houses, mostly red and many of them tiled; a
number of fine trees clustered about the manse
and the kirkyard, and turning the chief street
into a shady alley; many little gardens more than
usually bright with flowers; nets a-drying, and
fisher-wives scolding in the backward parts; a
smell of fish, a genial smell of seaweed; whiffs of

[2] From "Across the Plains With Other Memories and Essays." Copyright, 1892, by Charles Scribner's Sons.

blowing sand at the street-corners; shops with
golf-balls and bottled lollipops; another shop with
penny pickwicks (that remarkable cigar) and the
London *Journal*, dear to me for its startling pictures, and a few novels, dear for their suggestive
names: such, as well as memory serves me, were
the ingredients of the town. These, you are to
conceive, posted on a split between two sandy
bays, and sparsely flanked with villas—enough for
the boys to lodge in with their subsidiary parents,
not enough (not yet enough) to cocknify the
scene: a haven in the rocks in front: in front of
that, a file of gray islets: to the left, endless links
and sand wreaths, a wilderness of hiding-holes,
alive with popping rabbits and soaring gulls: to
the right, a range of seaward crags, one rugged
brow beyond another; the ruins of a mighty and
ancient fortress on the brink of one; coves between—now charmed into sunshine quiet, now
whistling with wind and clamorous with bursting
surges; the dens and sheltered hollows redolent of
thyme and southernwood, the air at the cliff's
edge brisk and clean and pungent of the sea—in
front of all, the Bass Rock, tilted seaward.

There was nothing to mar your days, if you
were a boy summering in that part, but the em-
barrassment of pleasure. You might golf if you
wanted; but I seem to have been better employed.
You might secrete yourself in the Lady's Walk, a
certain sunless dingle of elders, all mossed over
by the damp as green as grass, and dotted here
and there by the stream-side with roofless walls,
the cold homes of anchorites. To fit themselves
for life, and with a special eye to acquire the art
of smoking, it was even common for the boys to

harbor there; and you might have seen a single penny pickwick, honestly shared in lengths with a blunt knife, bestrew the glen with these apprentices. Again, you might join our fishing parties, where we sat perched as thick as solan geese, a covey of little anglers, boy and girl, angling over each other's head, to the much entanglement of lines and loss of podleys and consequent shrill recrimination—shrill as the geese themselves. Indeed, had that been all, you might have done this often; but tho fishing be a fine pastime, the podley is scarce to be regarded as a dainty for the table; and it was a point of honor that a boy should eat all that he had taken. Or again, you might climb the Law, where the whale's jawbone stood landmark in the buzzing wind, and behold the face of many counties, and the smoke and spires of many towns, and the sails of distant ships. You might bathe, now in the flaws of fine weather, that we pathetically call our summer, now in a gale of wind, with the sand scouring your bare hide, your clothes thrashing abroad from underneath their guardian stone, the froth of the great breakers casting you headlong ere it had drowned your knees. Or you might explore the tidal rocks, above all in the ebb of springs, when the very roots of the hills were for the nonce discovered; following my leader from one group to another, groping in slippery tangle for the wreck of ships, wading in pools after the abominable creatures of the sea, and ever with an eye cast backward on the march of the tide and the menaced line of your retreat. And then you might go Crusoeing, a word that covers all extempore eating in the open air; digging perhaps a house under the margin of the links, kindling a fire of the sea-ware, and cooking apples there—if they were truly apples, for I sometimes suppose the merchant must have played us off with some inferior and quite local fruit, capable of resolving, in the neighborhood of fire, into mere sand and smoke and iodin; or perhaps pushing to Tantallon, you might lunch on sandwiches and visions in the grassy court, while the wind hummed in the crumbling turrets; or clambering along the coasts, ear geans[3] (the worst, I must suppose, in Christendom) from an adventurous gean tree that had taken root under a cliff, where it was shaken with an ague of east wind, and silvered after gales with salt, and grew so foreign among its bleak surroundings that to eat of its produce was an adventure in itself.

These are things that I recall with interest; but what my memory dwells upon the most, I have been all this while withholding. It was a sport peculiar to the place, and indeed to a week or so of our two months' holiday there. Maybe it still flourishes in its native spot; for boys and their pastimes are swayed by periodic forces inscrutable to man; so that tops and marbles reappear in their due season, regular like the sun and moon; and the harmless art of knucklebones has seen the fall of the Roman empire and the rise of the United States. It may still flourish in its native spot, but nowhere else, I am persuaded; for I tried myself to introduce it on Tweedside, and was defeated lamentably; its charm being quite local, like a country wine that cannot be exported.

[3] Wild cherries.

The idle manner of it was this:

Toward the end of September, when school-time was drawing near and the nights were already black, we would begin to sally from our respective villas, each equipped with a tin bull's-eye lantern. The thing was so well known that it had worn a rut in the commerce of Great Britain; and the grocers, about the due time, began to garnish their windows with our particular brand of luminary. We wore them buckled to the waist upon a cricket belt, and over them, such was the rigor of the game, a buttoned top-coat. They smelled noisomely of blistered tin; they never burned aright, though they would always burn our fingers; their use was naught; the pleasure of them merely fanciful; and yet a boy with a bull's-eye under his top-coat asked for nothing more. The fishermen used lanterns about their boats, and it was from them, I suppose, that we had got the hint; but theirs were not bull's-eyes, nor did we ever play at being fishermen. The police carried them at their belts, and we had plainly copied them in that; yet we did not pretend to be policemen. Burglars, indeed, we may have had some haunting thoughts of; and we had certainly an eye to past ages when lanterns were more common, and to certain story-books in which we had found them to figure very largely. But take it for all in all, the pleasure of the thing was substantive; and to be a boy with a bull's-eye under his top-coat was good enough for us.

When two of these asses met, there would be an anxious "Have you got your lantern?" and a gratified "Yes!" That was the shibboleth, and very needful too; for, as it was the rule to keep our glory contained, none could recognize a lantern-bearer, unless (like the pole-cat) by the smell. Four or five would sometimes climb into the belly of a ten-man lugger, with nothing but the thwarts above them—for the cabin was usually locked, or choose out some hollow of the links where the wind might whistle overhead. There the coats would be unbuttoned and the bull's-eyes discovered; and in the chequering glimmer, under the huge windy hall of the night, and cheered by a rich steam of toasting tinware, these fortunate young gentlemen would crouch together in the cold sand of the links or on the scaly bilges of the fishing-boat, and delight themselves with inappropriate talk. Wo is me that I may not give some specimens—some of their foresights of life, or deep inquiries into the rudiments of man and nature, these were so fiery and so innocent, they were so richly silly, so romantically young. But the talk, at any rate, was but a condiment; and these gatherings themselves only accidents in the career of the lantern-bearer. The essence of this bliss was to walk by yourself in the black night; the slide shut, the top-coat buttoned; not a ray escaping, whether to conduct your footsteps or to make your glory public: a mere pillar of darkness in the dark; and all the while deep down in the privacy of your fool's heart, to know you had a bull's-eye at your belt, and to exult and sing over the knowledge.

END OF VOL. VI.